657

D0247308

AAT

Accounts

Preparation

Level 3

Advanced Diploma in

Accounting

Course Book

Central Beds College LRC

10050330

CENTRAL BEDS COLLEGE
LIBRARY

Fourth edition 2018

ISBN 9781 5097 1830 6
ISBN (for internal use only) 9781 5097 1824 5

British Library Cataloguing-in-Publication Data
A catalogue record for this book is available from the
British Library

Published by

BPP Learning Media Ltd
BPP House, Aldine Place
142-144 Uxbridge Road
London W12 8AA

www.bpp.com/learningmedia

Printed in the United Kingdom

> Your learning materials, published by BPP Learning Media
> Ltd, are printed on paper obtained from traceable
> sustainable sources.

All rights reserved. No part of this publication may be
reproduced, stored in a retrieval system or transmitted in any
form or by any means, electronic, mechanical,
photocopying, recording or otherwise, without the prior
written permission of BPP Learning Media.

The contents of this course material are intended as a guide
and not professional advice. Although every effort has been
made to ensure that the contents of this course material are
correct at the time of going to press, BPP Learning Media
makes no warranty that the information in this course
material is accurate or complete and accept no liability for
any loss or damage suffered by any person acting or
refraining from acting as a result of the material in this
course material.

BPP Learning Media is grateful to the IASB for permission to
reproduce extracts from the International Financial Reporting
Standards including all International Accounting Standards,
SIC and IFRIC Interpretations (the Standards). The Standards
together with their accompanying documents are issued by:

The International Accounting Standards Board (IASB) 30
Cannon Street, London, EC4M 6XH, United Kingdom. Email:
info@ifrs.org Web: www.ifrs.org

Disclaimer: The IASB, the International Financial Reporting
Standards (IFRS) Foundation, the authors and the publishers
do not accept responsibility for any loss caused by acting or
refraining from acting in reliance on the material in this
publication, whether such loss is caused by negligence or
otherwise to the maximum extent permitted by law.

©
BPP Learning Media Ltd
2018

A note about copyright

Dear Customer

What does the little © mean and why does it matter?

Your market-leading BPP books, course materials and e-
learning materials do not write and update themselves.
People write them on their own behalf or as employees of
an organisation that invests in this activity. Copyright law
protects their livelihoods. It does so by creating rights over
the use of the content.

Breach of copyright is a form of theft – as well as being a
criminal offence in some jurisdictions, it is potentially a
serious breach of professional ethics.

With current technology, things might seem a bit hazy but,
basically, without the express permission of BPP Learning
Media:

- Photocopying our materials is a breach of copyright

- Scanning, ripcasting or conversion of our digital
  materials into different file formats, uploading them
  to facebook or e-mailing them to your friends is a
  breach of copyright

You can, of course, sell your books, in the form in which
you have bought them – once you have finished with
them. (Is this fair to your fellow students? We update for a
reason.) Please note the e-products are sold on a single
user licence basis: we do not supply 'unlock' codes to
people who have bought them secondhand.

And what about outside the UK? BPP Learning Media
strives to make our materials available at prices students
can afford by local printing arrangements, pricing policies
and partnerships which are clearly listed on our website.
A tiny minority ignore this and indulge in criminal activity
by illegally photocopying our material or supporting
organisations that do. If they act illegally and unethically
in one area, can you really trust them?

Copyright © IFRS Foundation

All rights reserved. Reproduction and use rights are strictly
limited. No part of this publication may be translated,
reprinted or reproduced or utilised in any form either in
whole or in part or by any electronic, mechanical or other
means, now known or hereafter invented, including
photocopying and recording, or in any information
storage and retrieval system, without prior permission in
writing from the IFRS Foundation. Contact the IFRS
Foundation for further details.

The IFRS Foundation logo, the IASB logo, the IFRS for
SMEs logo, the "Hexagon Device", "IFRS Foundation",
"eIFRS", "IAS", "IASB", "IFRS for SMEs", "IASs", "IFRS",
"IFRSs", "International Accounting Standards" and
"International Financial Reporting Standards", "IFRIC"
"SIC" and "IFRS Taxonomy" are **Trade Marks** of the
IFRS Foundation.

Further details of the Trade Marks including details of
countries where the Trade Marks are registered or applied
for are available from the Licensor on request.

BPP
LEARNING MEDIA

Contents

Introduction to the course

Syllabus overview

This Advanced level unit is about preparing final accounts for sole traders and partnerships, and helping students to become aware of alternative business organisation structures.

This purpose of this unit is to provide the background knowledge and skills that a student needs in order to be capable of drafting accounts for sole traders and partnerships, and it provides the background knowledge of the regulations governing company accounts. A successful student will be able to complete tasks while being aware of potential ethical issues and know how to report information effectively.

Final Accounts Preparation is a mandatory unit in this qualification. It is closely linked to the Advanced level financial accounting unit, *Advanced Bookkeeping*, as well as to the Foundation level units, *Bookkeeping Transactions* and *Bookkeeping Controls*. In addition, it draws on the ethical principles from the Advanced level unit, *Ethics for Accountants*. On completion of this unit, students are prepared to start the Professional level unit, *Financial Statements of Limited Companies*.

It is recommended that this unit is taken after *Advanced Bookkeeping* and with or after *Ethics for Accountants*.

Test specification for this unit assessment

Assessment method	Marking type	Duration of assessment
Computer based assessment	Computer marked	2 hours

Learning outcomes		Weighting
1	Distinguish between the financial recording and reporting requirements of different types of organisation	10%
2	Explain the need for final accounts and the accounting and ethical principles underlying their preparation	7%
3	Prepare accounting records from incomplete information	27%
4	Produce accounts for sole traders	31%
5	Produce accounts for partnerships	20%
6	Recognise the key differences between preparing accounts for a limited company and a sole trader	5%
Total		**100%**

BPP LEARNING MEDIA

Assessment structure

2 hours duration

Competency is 70%

*Note that this is only a guideline as to what might come up. The format and content of each task may vary from what we have listed below.

Your assessment will consist of 6 tasks

Task	Expected content	Max marks	Chapter ref	Study complete
Task 1	**Reconstructing general ledger accounts** Reconstruction of ledger accounts, sales and purchases ledger control accounts, sales tax control accounts and the bank account using the content of daybooks and the cash book. Students may be required to distinguish between relevant and non-relevant data, calculate and correctly label the missing figure of reconstructed accounts, and calculate opening and closing balances from information given.	15	Incomplete records	
Task 2	**Incomplete records and applying ethical principles when preparing final accounts** Students may be asked possible reasons why information may be missing, or reasons for inconsistencies. Students may have to calculate mark up and margin and use that information to calculate missing figures, and to use cost of goods sold to determine a missing figure. Students may also be required to understand the importance of behaving professionally and being competent.	15	Incomplete records, Organisations and their final accounts	

BPP LEARNING MEDIA

Task	Expected content	Max marks	Chapter ref	Study complete
Task 3	**Final accounts for sole traders** Students may be given trial balance and asked to prepare a statement of profit or loss, or statement of financial position for a sole trader. Students may be asked some additional questions which demonstrate their understanding of how the statement of financial position is linked to the accounting equation, or how the statement of profit or loss and the statement of financial position are related, or other matters related to the final accounts of sole traders.	18	Accounts for sole traders	
Task 4	**The knowledge and understanding underpinning final accounts preparation** Students will be required to answer a number of theory questions about the preparation of final accounts. Students will need to know the primary users of final accounts and why they are needed by those users. Questions are likely to be asked about the existence of a framework within which accountants work, the underlying assumptions of financial statements as well as the fundamental qualitative characteristics and supporting qualitative characteristics of useful financial information.	16	Organisations and their final accounts, Introduction to limited company statements.	
Task 5	**Accounting for partnerships** Students will be required to answer questions about partnership agreements and other theory questions related to the preparation of partnership accounts. Other tasks likely to be included here are the preparation of goodwill and appropriation accounts for partnerships.	15	Accounts for partnerships	

BPP
LEARNING MEDIA

Task	Expected content	Max marks	Chapter ref	Study complete
Task 6	**Final accounts for partnerships and an introduction to reporting regulations for a limited company** Students will be required to prepare the statement of profit or loss, or the statement of financial position of a partnership from a given trial balance. Students may also be required to do some additional calculations pertaining to partnership accounts, such as partners' current accounts. Finally, students should expect to answer a question about the reporting regulations of a limited company.	21	Accounts for partnerships, Introduction to limited company accounts.	

Skills bank

Our experience of preparing students for this type of assessment suggests that to obtain competency, you will need to develop a number of key skills.

What do I need to know to do well in the assessment?

This Level 3 unit is about the student being able to prepare final accounts for sole traders and partnerships, and becoming aware of alternative business organisation structures.

This purpose of this unit is to provide the background knowledge and skills a student needs to be capable of drafting accounts for sole traders and partnerships and provides the background knowledge of the regulations governing company accounts. Successful students will be able to complete tasks while being aware of potential ethical issues and know how to report information effectively. Able to work with little supervision, the student should become an accomplished member of the accounting team, seeing a financial picture of the organisation as a whole.

Assumed knowledge

Final Accounts Preparation is a **mandatory** unit. It is closely linked to the Level 3 financial accounting unit *Advanced Bookkeeping*, as well as to the Level 2 units, *Bookkeeping Transactions* and *Bookkeeping Controls*. In addition, it draws on the ethical principles from the Level 3 unit *Ethics for Accountants*. On completion of this unit, students are prepared to start the Level 4 unit *Financial Statements of Limited Companies*.

It is recommended that this unit is taken after *Advanced Bookkeeping* and with or after *Ethics for Accountants*.

Assessment style

In the assessment you will complete tasks by:

1   Entering narrative by selecting from drop down menus of narrative options known as **picklists**

2   Using **drag and drop** menus to enter narrative

3   Typing in numbers, known as **gapfill** entry

4   Entering **ticks**

5   Entering **dates** by selecting from a calendar

You must familiarise yourself with the style of the online questions and the AAT software before taking the assessment. As part of your revision, login to the **AAT website** and attempt their **online practice assessments**.

BPP
LEARNING MEDIA

Introduction to the assessment

The question practice you do will prepare you for the format of tasks you will see in the *Final Accounts Preparation* assessment. It is also useful to familiarise yourself with the introductory information you **may** be given at the start of the assessment. For example:

You have 2 hours to complete this assessment.

This assessment contains 6 tasks and you should attempt to complete every task.

Each task is independent. You will not need to refer to your answers to previous tasks.

Read every task carefully to make sure you understand what is required.

The standard rate of VAT is 20%.

Where the date is relevant, it is given in the task data.

Both minus signs and brackets can be used to indicate negative numbers unless task instructions say otherwise.

You must use a full stop to indicate a decimal point. For example, write 100.57 not 100,57 or 100 57.

You may use a comma to indicate a number in the thousands, but you don't have to. For example, 10000 and 10,000 are both OK.

---

1   As you revise, use the **BPP Passcards** to consolidate your knowledge. They are a pocket-sized revision tool, perfect for packing in that last-minute revision.

2   Attempt as many tasks as possible in the **Question Bank**. There are plenty of assessment-style tasks which are excellent preparation for the real assessment.

3   Always **check** through your own answers as you will in the real assessment, before looking at the solutions in the back of the Question Bank.

Key to icons

 Key term

A key definition which is important to be aware of for the assessment

 Formula to learn

A formula you will need to learn as it will not be provided in the assessment

 Formula provided

A formula which is provided within the assessment and generally available as a pop-up on screen

 Activity

An example which allows you to apply your knowledge to the technique covered in the Course Book. The solution is provided at the end of the chapter

 Illustration

A worked example which can be used to review and see how an assessment question could be answered

 Assessment focus point

A high priority point for the assessment

Open book reference

Where use of an open book will be allowed for the assessment

Real life examples

A practical real life scenario

BPP
LEARNING MEDIA

AAT qualifications

The material in this book may support the following AAT qualifications:

AAT Advanced Diploma in Accounting Level 3, AAT Advanced Diploma in Accounting at SCQF Level 6 and Further Education and Training Certificate: Accounting Technician (Level 4 AATSA)

Supplements

From time to time we may need to publish supplementary materials to one of our titles. This can be for a variety of reasons, from a small change in the AAT unit guidance to new legislation coming into effect between editions.

You should check our supplements page regularly for anything that may affect your learning materials. All supplements are available free of charge on our supplements page on our website at:

www.bpp.com/learning-media/about/students

Improving material and removing errors

There is a constant need to update and enhance our study materials in line with both regulatory changes and new insights into the assessments.

From our team of authors BPP appoints, a subject expert to update and improve these materials for each new edition.

Their updated draft is subsequently technically checked by another author and from time to time non-technically checked by a proof reader.

We are very keen to remove as many numerical errors and narrative typos as we can but given the volume of detailed information being changed in a short space of time we know that a few errors will sometimes get through our net.

We apologise in advance for any inconvenience that an error might cause. We continue to look for new ways to improve these study materials and would welcome your suggestions. Please feel free to contact our AAT Head of Programme at nisarahmed@bpp.com if you have any suggestions for us.

BPP
LEARNING MEDIA

Organisations and their final accounts

1

Learning outcomes

1.1	**Describe the types of organisation that need to prepare final accounts**
	• Know brief descriptions of business organisations:
	– For profit: sole traders, partnerships, limited companies, limited liability partnerships (LLPs)
	– Not-for-profit: charities
	• The basic differences between the structure and financial characteristics of these organisations:
	– Who own the organisation/public benefit requirement
	– Who manages the organisation
	– Where responsibility for debts the organisation cannot pay lies, and the amount of exposure
	– Whether, and how, any tax is paid
	• For commercial organisations, the different terms used to represent ownership in the statement of financial position (capital and equity) and amounts taken by the owners (drawings and dividends)
	• For charity organisations, representation of net assets in the statement of financial position as funds of the charity
	• Recognise basic advantages and disadvantages of operating as a partnership rather than a sole trader
	• Recognise basic advantages and disadvantages of incorporated status

1.2	**Recognise the regulations applying to different types of organisation**
	• Know that different regulations apply to different organisations, including awareness of relevant:
	– Partnership legislation
	– Companies legislation and accounting standards
	– Limited liability partnership legislation
	– Charity legislation, charity regulators and statements of recommended practice
	• Know that presentation of final accounts for sole traders and partnerships is not governed by statute and accounting regulations to the same extent those for limited companies are; they have no definitive format
	• Know the importance of behaving professionally, being competent and acting with due care at work
	• Know the importance of deadlines in the preparation of final accounts.
2.3	**Apply ethical principles when preparing final accounts**
	• Know the importance of behaving professionally and being competent
	• Know the importance of objectivity, including awareness of the potential for conflicts of interest and bias
	• Know why security and confidentiality of information must be maintained at all times

Assessment context

Questions on this area will be tested in Tasks 2 and 4 of the exam and throughout the exam in theory elements of other questions.

Qualification context

The regulatory framework of financial statements is examined throughout your AAT studies.

Business context

The preparation of accounts for different types of organisation is the main source of revenue for a lot of smaller accountancy practices. An understanding of the regulatory framework is essential in order to complete the relevant returns in a timely fashion.

BPP
LEARNING MEDIA

Chapter overview

Organisations and their final accounts

Sole trader

- Owns and manages business
- No requirement to file annual returns
- Unlimited liability
- Taxed as individual

Partnership

- Partners own and manage the business
- No requirement to file annual returns, but must produce year-end accounts
- Unlimited liability unless LLP
- Taxed as individuals

Limited company

- Separation of ownership and management
- Annual returns must be filed
- Limited liability
- Company tax must be paid
- Must comply with Companies Act

Note. A not-for-profit organisation can be any of the above.

Introduction

This unit will teach you how to prepare final accounts for sole traders and partnerships. In order to do that, there is a certain amount of background knowledge required. This chapter will introduce you to alternative business organisation structures, which are then expanded on in later chapters.

When you complete tasks, and prepare final accounts, you should do so while being aware of potential ethical issues. Knowledge of how to report information effectively is also important.

1 The different types of organisation

There are several types of organisation:

Sole traders: a business owned and managed by one person

Partnerships: a business owned and managed by two or more people

Limited liability partnership: a business owned and managed by two or more people, but partners have limited liability

Companies: a business that is a **separate legal entity** from its owners

Not-for-profit: a business which is not conducted primarily to make a profit (eg a charity)

For the purpose of preparing financial statements, a business is always treated as being separate from its owners.

1.1 Unincorporated entities

Sole traders and partnerships are unincorporated entities. This means that there is no legal distinction between the business and its owners. Consequently, sole traders and partners have **unlimited liability**.

Therefore, if the business does not have the resources to pay its liabilities the owners must meet the claims against the business.

Sole traders and partnerships are not legally required to produce or file annual accounts, but will need to keep records in order to complete tax returns.

Tax does not appear in the accounts of unincorporated businesses as the owners are taxed personally on the profits of the business.

1.2 Incorporated entities

A company is a separate legal entity. It can enter into contracts, acquire assets and incur liabilities in its own right. A limited company must prepare and file annual accounts each year. A copy must be filed at Companies House and a copy sent to all shareholders.

BPP
LEARNING MEDIA

'Limited company' means that the liability of the owners of the company is limited to their investment in the company. As the company is a separate legal entity, should the business fail and be liquidated, the maximum amount that the owners lose is the amount of capital they have agreed to invest in the company.

The owners of a company are called shareholders. Each shareholder must own at least one share in the company.

There are two types of companies, **public limited companies** (plc) and **private limited companies** (Ltd).

Public limited companies: may raise capital from the public on the stock exchange, although they do not have to.

Private limited companies: cannot invite the general public to invest in their shares through a stock exchange.

As companies are separate legal entities, they are taxed in their own right. Therefore, tax will appear in the financial statements of limited companies.

If the partners of a partnership don't want to be personally responsible for the business's losses, they can set up a limited partnership or limited liability partnership (LLP). LLP members are self-employed for tax purposes, and the LLP itself is not taxed as a whole. The main difference between an LLP and a traditional partnership is the limited liability of each partner. The LLP is an individual person in the eyes of the law and can enter into contracts in its own name, and is therefore responsible for its own debts and liabilities. The members are only responsible for what they invest or agree to contribute towards the LLP's debts.

1.3 Owners and managers

Sole traders and partners normally own and manage their business themselves. They take **drawings** from the business for their personal expenses. In a partnership, the partnership agreement will set out the agreed share of profits between the partners.

Limited companies (particularly the large ones) are often managed by persons other than their owners. Shareholders will be paid dividends, based on the profits earned by the company.

- **Shareholders** (owners) will invest in the business but are not involved in the day-to-day running of the company.

- **Directors** are appointed to manage the company on behalf of the shareholders.

As shareholders are not involved in the running of the business day to day, they need a way of evaluating the performance of the directors. The financial statements enable them to assess the way in which the directors are safeguarding the assets of the company and using them to generate profits (stewardship of management).

1.4 Advantages and disadvantages

Now we will recap by looking at the advantages and disadvantages of these forms of organisation.

A sole trader considering taking on one or more partners will have to consider the following:

1.4.1 Advantages of partnership over sole proprietorship

(a) There will be more than one individual contributing funds.

(b) The partners will bring in different areas of expertise – for instance one partner may have a manufacturing or engineering background and another may be experienced in sales.

(c) Further partners can be brought in to obtain additional capital or needed expertise.

(d) There will be more than one person contributing ideas and helping to solve problems.

1.4.2 Disadvantages of partnership

(a) Partners may have different and conflicting ideas. This can lead to disagreements and disputes.

(b) If a partner wants to retire the partnership has to find the money to repay their capital.

(c) A certain amount of regulation applies. Partnerships in the UK are established under the Partnership Act. There must be a partnership agreement specifying profit share and, at the year end, accounts must be produced and profit or loss shared. Records must be kept of partners' drawings.

A sole proprietor or partnership may be considering incorporation and will have to look at the following:

1.4.3 Advantages of incorporation

(a) Limited liability. If a company goes into liquidation the shareholders are only liable for any amount unpaid on their shares. A sole trader or partner will be personally responsible for any outstanding debts.

(b) Companies find it easier to obtain funds than unincorporated entities. Larger companies can issue loan stock. Companies can also raise further capital by share issues.

(c) If a listed company is profitable and expanding, its share price can be expected to rise. Shareholders therefore have the opportunity to realise a capital gain on their investment.

BPP
LEARNING MEDIA

1.4.4 Disadvantages of incorporation

(a) A company faces a much greater regulatory burden than an unincorporated entity. It must produce accounts each year and file its return and accounts with the Registrar of Companies. It must comply with the Companies Act.

(b) A large company is required to have an annual audit, which is costly.

(c) Owners of the company (shareholders) may have little chance of influencing the day-to-day management of the business.

Activity 1: Partnerships

Which of the following statements is correct?

	✓
Partnerships have a legal obligation to produce annual accounts.	
Partners are paid dividends from the partnership profits.	
Some partnerships have limited liability.	
Partnerships can issue loan stock to raise money.	

Activity 2: Incorporation

Which of the following is an advantage of incorporation for a sole proprietor?

	✓
The sole proprietor will no longer have to pay personal tax.	
The sole proprietor will have greater control of the business.	
The business will operate in compliance with the Companies Act.	
The sole proprietor has more protection in the event of a liquidation.	

Activity 3: Limited companies

Which of the following statements regarding limited liability is correct?

	✓
A company may only have a certain prescribed maximum liability on its statement of financial position.	
The shareholders of a company are protected in that they can only lose their investment in the company, should the company fail.	
A company can only enter into transactions involving debt up to a certain limit before gaining express approval from the shareholders in general meeting.	
The shareholders may only invest in a company up to a prescribed limit per shareholder.	

2 Companies Act 2006

As already mentioned, all UK registered companies must comply with the Companies Act 2006.

The Companies Act contains many provisions relating to the formation, governance and administration of a company. For this course, you are only required to know the provisions relating to the duties and responsibilities of directors.

The Companies Act is legally binding in the UK. Therefore, contravening it is a criminal offence which may result in the directors or other responsible parties receiving penalties in the form of a fine and/or imprisonment.

2.1 Duties and responsibilities of the directors

The directors are responsible for keeping proper company accounting records.

They are also responsible for preparing the company's annual financial statements, having them audited (if the company is of a certain size) and presenting them to the shareholders in a general meeting.

The shareholders must approve the financial statements at the general meeting and then the directors are responsible for filing them with the Registrar of Companies. You may have heard this organisation referred to as Companies House.

The directors must ensure the accounts are filed with the Registrar of Companies within the prescribed period after year end.

BPP
LEARNING MEDIA

2.2 True and fair view

The financial statements must show a true and fair view of the company's results for the period and its assets and liabilities at the end of the period.

Note that companies have to meet **filing deadlines** in respect of their financial statements and that partnerships have to produce accounts as soon as possible after the year end so that profits can be shared.

Accountants must therefore work competently and meet deadlines in preparation of the final accounts.

2.3 Not-for-profit organisations

Not-for-profit organisations have objectives which are quite distinct in many respects.

For example:

- They do not report to shareholders (but may have stakeholders)
- Focus is often on cash flow and income generation rather than profit
- They do not normally pay dividends

Examples of not-for-profit organisations:

- Charities
- Clubs and societies
- Non-governmental organisations (NGOs)

A charity in the UK is granted its charitable status by the Charity Commission. It must pass the 'public benefit' test – it must be established and operate for the general public's benefit, not simply for the benefit of its members or employees.

Charities are regulated by accounting standards, charity law, relevant company law and best practice. In addition to a statement of financial position, charities produce a statement of financial activities (SOFA), an Annual Report to the Charity Commission and sometimes an income and expenditure account. The SOFA is the primary statement showing the results of the charity's activities for the period. The organisation will also produce a statement of financial position which will show the total of the charity's funds from all sources as equal to the net assets.

The Charity Commission is responsible for issuing the statement of recommended practice (SORP) for charities. The SORP for charities supplements the regular accounting standards and other legal and regulatory requirements in light of special factors relating to charities.

Activity 4: Duties and responsibilities of the directors

The following statements refer to actions that may be required in relation to companies.

(i)   Enter into contracts on behalf of the company
(ii)   File the financial statements on time
(iii)   Prepare proper accounting records
(iv)   Present the financial statements to be audited (if applicable)

Which of the above statements are duties of a director?

	✓
(ii), (iii) and (iv)	
(i), (ii), (iii) and (iv)	
(i), (iii) and (iv)	
(i), (ii) and (iii)	

3 Limited liability partnerships (LLPs)

The Limited Liability Partnership Act 2000 (LLPA 2000) allowed the formation of a new type of legal trading entity, the Limited Liability Partnership. Despite the name, LLPs have much more in common with companies than standard partnerships.

The key features of an LLP include:

(a)   Must be registered with the Registrar of Companies, with formation documents signed by at least two members

(b)   The name of the partnership must end with LLP

(c)   Partners are known as **members**, of which there must be at least two (no upper limit applies)

(d)   The partnership **must file** annual returns and accounts; where applicable, an audit is also required

(e)   The LLP is a **separate legal entity** with all of the associated features this entails

(f)   **Members are agents** of the LLP, and can bind in the same way as partners in a standard partnership

(g)   **Members' liability is limited** to an amount stated in the partnership document (no lower limit exists)

(h)   **Designated members** are responsible for administration and filing

BPP
LEARNING MEDIA

(i) The LLP is not subject to **corporation tax**; the members therefore enjoy the same taxable status as partners of a standard partnership

(j) The LLP must comply with applicable provisions of the Companies Act

4 Professional ethics

4.1 Professions

A profession is an occupation that requires extensive training and the study and mastery of specialised knowledge, and usually has a professional association, ethical code and process of certification or licensing.

4.2 Codes

Professional bodies will issue **'Codes of Conduct'** or **'Codes of Ethics'**, which members are expected to adhere to. These may be developed using one of two approaches:

(a) A **rules-based approach = prescriptive**, creating specific rules for members to follow in as many situations as possible

(b) A **framework-based approach = values and qualities**, describing fundamental values and qualities that members should aspire to, but not laying out prescriptive rules

4.3 Difference between approaches

The difference between the two approaches can be demonstrated by considering the discipline procedures for employees of most companies. Serious offences, such as violence, drinking and drug offences, are always treated as gross misconduct and immediate dismissal. They are always wrong, and therefore punished. This is an example of a rules-based approach. Other offences such as time keeping go through more stages and the reasons are investigated (childcare issues vs lazy); discretion is then applied. Whether the offence is wrong or not depends on the circumstances and perhaps the consequences. This is an example of a framework-based approach.

5 A code of ethics for accountants

5.1 International Ethics Standards Board

Accountancy is a high-profile profession and accountants are frequently in positions of trust and responsibility. A code of ethics for accountants has been issued by the **International Ethics Standards Board (IESBA)**, whose work is facilitated by the International Federation of Accountants (IFAC). This code has formed the basis for the AAT *Code of Professional Ethics*. Principles of the code include:

(a) **Integrity** – acting with truthfulness and honesty

(b) **Objectivity** – reaching conclusions without undue influence or bias

(c) **Professional competence and due care** – maintaining a high level of skill and knowledge

(d) **Confidentiality** – not sharing confidential information, unless terrorism or money laundering is suspected for example

(e) **Professional behaviour** – behaving in a way that does not bring the institute into disrepute

(AAT, 2014)

5.2 AAT students and members

To meet these principles, students and members of the AAT need to develop a mix of personal and professional qualities.

Personal qualities include:

(a) Reliability – all work must meet professional standards
(b) Responsibility – taking ownership for your work
(c) Timeliness – delays can be costly and disruptive
(d) Courtesy – to colleagues and clients
(e) Respect – to develop constructive relationships

Professional qualities include:

(a) Independence – not only being independent, but also appearing to be independent

(b) Scepticism – questioning information and data

(c) Accountability – for judgements and decisions

(d) Social responsibility – to your employer and the public

6 Threats to independence and conflicts of interest

The IESBA Code outlines the threats to an accountant's independence that could arise in a variety of situations. These are:

(a) **Self-interest threat**

Occurs when a firm or a member of the assurance team has some financial or other interest in an assurance client, eg providing a loan to a client

(b) **Self-review threat**

Occurs when a previous judgement needs to be re-evaluated by members responsible for that judgement, eg providing a valuation for a client's pension liability and subsequently auditing the liability

(c) **Advocacy threat**

Occurs when members promote a position or opinion to the point that subsequent objectivity may be compromised, eg acting as an advocate on behalf of an assurance client in litigation or disputes with third parties

BPP
LEARNING MEDIA

(d) **Familiarity threat**

Occurs when, because of a close relationship, members become too sympathetic to the interests of others, eg long association with a client/boss leading to overfamiliarity with client/management such that professional judgement could be compromised

(e) **Intimidation threat**

Occurs when members are deterred from acting objectively by threats, actual or perceived, eg being pressured to reduce inappropriately the extent of work performed in order to reduce fees

(IESBA, 2015)

These threats can arise from many situations which accountants could find themselves facing. The following represent some instances of these threats in operation but is by no means an exhaustive list.

- Pressure from an overbearing colleague or from family or friends
- Members asked to act contrary to technical and/or professional standards
- Divided loyalties between colleagues and professional standards
- Publication of misleading information
- Members having to do work beyond their degree of expertise or experience they possess
- Personal relationships with other employees or clients
- Gifts and hospitality being offered

7 Data protection and security

There is a risk that information about individuals and companies could be misused. It is felt that an individual or company could easily be harmed by the dissemination of data about the company which could be **transferred to unauthorised third parties**. This could lead to a loss of competitive advantage.

The **key risks** affecting data are:

(a) Human error
(b) Technical malfunction
(c) Deliberate/malicious action
(d) Hacking

Accountants should identify and mitigate these risks in order to protect their clients and other stakeholders.

Activity 5: Professional ethics

Indicate whether the following statements are true or false.

	True ✓	False ✓
Confidential information should only be shared with other accountants in your firm.		
The same audit team being sent to a client for several years can give rise to a familiarity threat.		
Gifts from clients can be accepted as long as they are valued below £100.		

Chapter summary

- There are several broad types of organisation:

  - Profit-making

    (1)   Sole traders
    (2)   Partnerships
    (3)   Companies

  - Not-for-profit

    (1)   Charities, clubs and societies
    (2)   Public sector organisations

- A limited company:

  - Has a separate legal personality from that of its owners
  - Gives its shareholders (owners) limited liability

- Limited liability means that the owners' liability is limited to the amount that they have paid for their shares. This is the maximum amount that they can lose if the company is wound up.

- Limited companies are owned by shareholders and managed by directors.

- Ethics have been defined as a set of moral principles which determine our perception of right and wrong. These are distinct from the legal rules that we have to comply with.

- Professional bodies including the AAT issue codes of practice adopting a rules-based approach or a framework-based approach. The IESBA Code forms the basis of the AAT Code and it covers both principles and qualities required of members of accountancy bodies.

Keywords

- **Sole trader:** A business owned and managed by one person
- **Partnership:** A business jointly owned and managed by two or more people
- **Company:** A business that is a separate legal entity from its owners
- **Entity:** Any organisation (whether profit making or not for profit) that prepares accounts as a separate entity from its owners
- **Public limited companies:** Companies that can invite members of the general public to invest in their shares
- **Private limited companies:** Companies that cannot invite members of the general public to invest in their shares
- **Not-for-profit entities:** Organisations whose business is not conducted primarily to make a profit

BPP
LEARNING MEDIA

Test your learning

1   **Indicate whether each of these organisations is profit making or not for profit.**

	Profit making ✓	Not for profit ✓
A restaurant		
A school		
A cinema		
A public library		
A local council		
The Red Cross		
A church		
A bank		
A public hospital		
A supermarket		
An accountancy firm		

2 **Complete the following sentences:**

(a) Sole traders and partnerships are [▼] entities.

(b) [▼] limited companies can raise capital on the stock exchange.

(c) Directors manage a company on behalf of the [▼].

(d) Duties and responsibilities of directors are set out in the [▼].

(e) The professional quality that requires an accountant to question information and data is [▼].

Picklist:

Companies Act
Conceptual Framework
Employees
Incorporated
Objectivity
Private
Public
Scepticism
Shareholders
Unincorporated

3 **Identify the four key risks to data security.**

	✓
Human error	
Lack of funds	
Hacking	
Malicious action	
Government interference	
Technical malfunction	
Intimidation	

BPP
LEARNING MEDIA

4 Which one of the following is true in respect of partnerships?

	✓
Ownership and management are separated.	
Partners have no personal liability for the firm's debts.	
Each partner receives an agreed percentage of the profits.	
Partnerships can issue loan stock.	

5 Your audit client has a yacht and has offered you a free holiday. This represents a threat to your professional independence.

How do we categorise this threat?

▼

Picklist:

Advocacy threat
Intimidation threat
Self-interest threat
Self-review threat

BPP
LEARNING MEDIA

Incomplete records

2

Learning outcomes

3.1	**Recognise circumstances where there are incomplete records**
	• Know possible reasons why information may be missing
	• Know possible reasons for inconsistencies within the records themselves
	• Provide examples of the types of figures that may be missing
	• Know the importance of acting with integrity
3.2	**Prepare ledger accounts, using these to estimate missing figures**
	• How to use the content of daybooks, including value added tax (VAT)
	• How to use information from the cash book
	• How to distinguish between relevant and non-relevant data
	• How to reconstruct ledger accounts: sales and purchases ledger control accounts, VAT control account and the bank account
	• How to calculate and correctly label the missing figure of such reconstructed accounts
	• How to calculate opening or closing balances from information given
	• How to adjust data for VAT, using information given
3.3	**Calculate figures using mark-up and margin**
	• Know what margin and mark-up are and the difference between them
	• Calculate mark-up and margin
	• Use mark-up and margin to calculate missing figures
	• Use cost of goods sold to determine a missing figure
	• Adjust data for VAT from data provided
3.4	**Assess the reasonableness of given figures within a particular context**
	• Recognise whether a figure is reasonable in a given context
	• Explain reasons behind the difference between an actual balance and a calculation
	• Exercise professional scepticism

Assessment context

Questions on this area will be tested in Tasks 1 and 2 of the exam. These tasks will require you to use incomplete records techniques in order to finding missing figures such as sales, purchases, closing inventories, profit and drawings.

Qualification context

Incomplete records are only examined in *Final Accounts Preparation*.

Business context

For a variety of reasons, smaller businesses may not always keep full accounting records. Their accountants will need to use alternative methods to derive the information required to prepare the final accounts. This includes calculating missing numbers using the accounting equation, profit margins and mark-ups, and using general ledger accounts.

BPP
LEARNING MEDIA

Chapter overview

Known financial information can be included in a general ledger account

The account can be balanced off and missing figures derived

The accounting equation expresses the statement of financial position as an equation

The accounting equation may be expressed as:

Assets – liabilities = capital

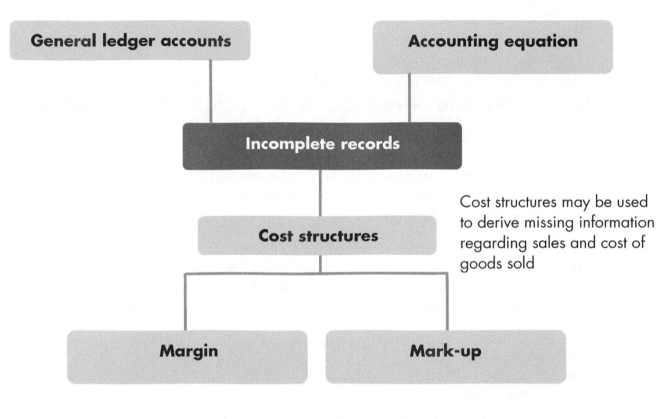

Cost structures may be used to derive missing information regarding sales and cost of goods sold

Gross profit expressed as a percentage of sales

For example, a 20% margin:

Sales	100%
Cost of goods sold	80%
Gross profit	20%

Gross profit expressed as a percentage of cost of goods sold

For example, a 25% margin:

Sales	125%
Cost of goods sold	100%
Gross profit	25%

Introduction

Owners running small businesses may not have the time or resources to keep full accounting records. Instead, only basic primary records may be maintained.

However, they still need to know how the business is performing and final accounts must be prepared.

There are several techniques that enable businesses to derive missing financial information from the available information:

- Deriving missing figures using general ledger accounts
- Deriving missing figures using a cost structure
- Using the accounting equation

These methods will be explained in this chapter.

1 Circumstances where there are incomplete records

1.1 Incomplete financial information

Individuals running small organisations, such as a newsagent or greengrocer, may not maintain detailed accounting records. Some financial transactions may be recorded in the general ledger but the accounting records may be incomplete.

However, the owners still need to know how the business is performing and produce final accounts. If some information is not recorded by the business, it will need to be derived from other available information. Information may also need to be derived where data has been lost or stolen.

1.2 Inconsistent financial information

Another circumstance which results in inconsistencies within the records themselves are errors in the accounting records.

From our previous studies, we know that similar financial transactions are categorised in the books of prime entry. The totals on the books of prime entry are then summarised and posted to the general ledger accounts.

At the period end, the closing balance of each general ledger account is used to extract an initial trial balance.

The trial balance should balance, ie total debits should equal total credits. If the trial balance does balance, it is less likely that errors have been made so the business can have reasonable confidence that it has processed its double entries correctly throughout the period.

However, it is still possible that the trial balance contains errors. There are various types of errors which can occur. Some errors still allow the trial balance to balance and others cause an imbalance in the trial balance.

BPP
LEARNING MEDIA

The following errors will still **allow the trial balance to balance**.

Type of error	Detail
Error of omission	Both sides of a transaction have been completely left out. For example, a rent payment of £800 is not recorded in the general ledger.
Error of original entry	An entry has been made so that debits = credits but the amount is incorrect. For example, a credit sale of £1,000 is posted as: DEBIT Sales ledger control account £150 CREDIT Sales £150
Reversal of entries	A transaction has been recorded at the correct amount but the debit and credit entries have been reversed. For example, the credit sale above is posted as: DEBIT Sales £1,000 CREDIT Sales ledger control account £1,000
Error of principle	Here debits = credits; however, one of the entries has been made to the wrong type of account. For example, £500 spent on repairing a motor vehicle has been recorded as: DEBIT Motor vehicles at cost £500 CREDIT Bank £500 Repairs are an item of expense which should be shown in the statement of profit or loss whereas the item has been recorded as a non-current asset.
Error of commission	Here debits = credits; however, one of the entries has been made to the wrong account, but not the wrong type of account. For example, £200 spent on telephone costs has been recorded as: DEBIT Insurance expense £200 CREDIT Bank £200 Both accounts (telephone and insurance costs) are expenses and so this is an error of commission rather than an error of principle.

BPP LEARNING MEDIA

The trial balance will not balance if total debits do not equal total credits. The following errors **cause an imbalance in the trial balance**:

Type of error	Detail
Unequal amounts error	Here an entry has been posted where debits ≠ credits. A common example of this is where a transposition error has been made and figures have been reversed. For example, £450 of rent costs have been posted as follows: DEBIT Rent £450 / CREDIT Bank £540 Here debits ≠ credits and so the trial balance will not balance.
Single entry error	Here a debit entry has been posted with no corresponding credit made or *vice versa*. For example, a credit sale of £300 has been posted as: DEBIT Sales ledger control account £300 or as: CREDIT Sales £300 Here debits ≠ credits and so the trial balance will not balance.
Two debits or two credits error	Here two debit entries or two credit entries have been posted. For example, the credit sale of £300 above has been posted as: DEBIT Sales ledger control account £300 / DEBIT Sales £300 or as: CREDIT Sales ledger control account £300 / CREDIT Sales £300 Here debits ≠ credits and so the trial balance will not balance.
Balance transfer error	Here the final balance on the general ledger account is incorrectly transferred to the trial balance. For example, a balance of £560 on the sales account was recorded in the trial balance as £650 or £400. Note that this type of error also includes the situation where the £560 balance on the sales account was completely omitted from the trial balance. Here debits ≠ credits and so the trial balance will not balance.

These errors will be corrected through journal entries.

BPP
LEARNING MEDIA

1.3 Integrity

As we have seen in the previous chapter, the *Code of Ethics* requires accountants to act with integrity. Reconstructing accounts from incomplete financial information is a sensitive task and, when performing this work, accountants must apply the principle of integrity.

This means that they must not present untruthful or misleading information. Instead, accounts must be reconstructed as completely and accurately as possible.

2 VAT – A reminder from the Level 2 accounting units

Assessment focus point

VAT was covered in the Level 2 accounting units and tested in those assessments. VAT does not play such an important part in the *Final Accounts Preparation* syllabus. However, questions on incomplete records may require knowledge of accounting for VAT.

The standard rate of VAT in all assessments is 20%.

If the sales of a business exceed a certain amount in a year then the business must register for VAT with the tax authorities. In the UK the tax authorities are HM Revenue & Customs (HMRC).

Registered businesses must:

- Charge VAT on sales (also known as output tax)
- Suffer VAT on purchases (also known as input tax)

This means that goods and services are sold to customers at the sales price plus the VAT. Generally, items appear more expensive than they would be without the VAT. However, registered businesses can recover VAT on purchases from the tax authorities.

To enable the business to identify the amount due to and recoverable from the tax authorities, the VAT amounts are analysed separately in the books of prime entry.

Illustration 1: Accounting for VAT

A sale for £3,000 plus VAT at 20% would therefore be recorded in the sales day book as follows:

Date 20X9	Details	Net £	VAT £	Total £
16 Aug	A Customer	3,000	600	3,600
	Total	3,000	600	3,600

It would be posted to the general ledger accounts using the double entry:

Account name	Debit £	Credit £
Sales ledger control account	3,600	
VAT control account		600
Sales		3,000

Similarly, a purchase for £2,000 plus VAT at 20% would be recorded in the purchases day book as follows:

Date 20X9	Details	Net £	VAT £	Total £
31 Aug	A Supplier	2,000	400	2,400
	Total	2,000	400	2,400

It would be posted to the general ledger accounts using the double entry:

Account name	Debit £	Credit £
Purchases	2,000	
VAT control account	400	
Purchases ledger control account		2,400

BPP
LEARNING MEDIA

These transactions would then be shown in the VAT control account as follows:

VAT control account

	£		£
Purchases	400	Sales	600
Balance c/d	200		
	600		600
		Balance b/d	200

The above account shows that the business owes HMRC VAT of £600 in relation to sales it has made, but is due back VAT of £400 which it has suffered on its purchases.

The closing balance of £200 shows that the business has a **liability** to pay over the net VAT due.

Having recapped the principles of VAT, we will now see how missing figures can be derived from other available information.

3 Deriving missing figures using general ledger accounts

3.1 Credit sales and the balance on the sales ledger control account

If the business does not keep a record of sales made on credit (ie it does not maintain a sales day book), this information can be derived from the opening and closing balances on the sales ledger control account (trade receivables) in conjunction with the figure for payments received.

Activity 1: Calculating sales as a missing figure

During the year ended 31 December 20X9, a business had the following balances on its sales ledger control account:

Balances as at	31 December 20X8 £	31 December 20X9 £
Trade receivables	1,447	1,928

Payments received from credit customers during the year totalled £39,204.

Required

Find the missing sales figure by preparing the sales ledger control account for the year ended 31 December 20X9.

Solution

Sales ledger control account

	£			£
	▼		▼	
	▼		▼	

Picklist:

Balance b/d
Balance c/d
Bank
Purchases
Sales

BPP
LEARNING MEDIA

Activity 2: Calculating contras, VAT amounts and cash balances

This task is about incomplete records and reconstructing general ledger accounts.

You are working on the accounting records of a sole trader for the year ended 30 June 20X9.

You have the following information:

Day book summaries	Goods £	VAT £	Total £
Sales	150,000	30,000	180,000
Purchases	80,000	16,000	96,000
All sales and purchases are on credit terms			

Balances as at	30 June 20X8 £	30 June 20X9 £
Trade receivables	22,000	47,800
Trade payables	29,500	34,600
VAT	5,780 credit	Not available
Bank	83,456 debit	Not available

Further information	Net £	VAT £	Total £
General expenses	11,750	2,350	14,100
Purchases	80,000	16,000	96,000

Receipts and payments recorded in the bank account comprise	£
Amounts from credit customers	140,300
Amounts to credit suppliers	88,900
Rental income	10,000
Wages	14,750
HMRC for VAT – payment	11,800
General expenses	14,100

Required

(a) Find the missing contra figure by preparing the sales ledger control account for the year ended 30 June 20X9.

Sales ledger control account

	£			£
▼		▼		
▼		▼		
▼		▼		

Picklist:

Balance b/d
Balance c/d
Bank
Contra
Sales day book

(b) Find the closing balance on the VAT control account for the year ended 30 June 20X9.

Note. **The business is not charged VAT on its rental income.**

VAT control account

	£			£
▼		▼		
▼		▼		
▼		▼		
▼		▼		

Picklist:

Balance b/d
Balance c/d
Bank
General expenses
Purchases day book
Sales day book

BPP
LEARNING MEDIA

The totals recorded in the cash book for the year ended 30 June 20X9 were:

Receipts	£	150,300
Payments	£	129,550

(c) **Assuming there are no year-end adjustments, what will be the opening balance in the cash book as at 1 July 20X9?**

£		▼

Picklist:

Debit

Credit

3.2 Reminder

Note that the bank statement shows the balance from the bank's point of view, whereas the cash book is from the business's point of view.

Therefore, should a question state the bank account balance is in credit, this means that there is a **debit** balance in the business's records.

Conversely, should a question state that the bank account balance is overdrawn, then there is a **credit** balance in the business's records.

3.3 Credit purchases and the balance on the purchases ledger control account

In the examples above, we studied the general ledger accounts relating to credit sales. A similar relationship exists between purchases of goods, the opening and closing balances on the purchases ledger control account (trade payables) and payments made to credit suppliers during the period.

Activity 3: Calculating purchases as a missing figure

During the year ended 31 March 20X9, a business had the following balances on its purchases ledger control account:

Balances as at	31 March 20X8 £	31 March 20X9 £
Trade payables	38,450	43,825

Payments made to credit suppliers during the year were £167,224 made from the bank account and £430 from the till.

Required

Find the missing purchases figure by preparing the purchases ledger control account for the year ended 31 March 20X9.

Solution

Purchases ledger control account

	£			£
▼		▼		
▼		▼		
▼		▼		

Picklist:

Balance b/d
Balance c/d
Bank
Cash
Purchases
Sales

Activity 4: Calculating missing figures in general ledger accounts

This task is about incomplete records and reconstructing general ledger accounts.

You are working on the accounts of a sole trader for the year ended 31 August 20X9.

The business is not registered for VAT.

You have the following information:

Receipts and payments recorded in the bank account include	£
Amounts from credit customers	50,424
Amounts to credit suppliers	27,432
Interest received	180
General expenses	7,700
Purchase of a new computer	600
Cash sales banked	14,440

Balances as at	31.8.X8 £	31.8.X9 £
Trade receivables	10,253	12,442
Trade payables	7,322	5,322
Closing inventory	9,213	7,321
Bank	923 debit	1,723 debit

BPP LEARNING MEDIA

You are also told that:

- All purchases of goods are on credit terms

- An irrecoverable debt of £210 was written off during the year

- An allowance for doubtful debts of £200 is to be introduced

- The proprietor draws £1,800 per month from the business bank account

- The proprietor transferred her own vehicle valued at £11,000 to the business during the year

- Computers costing over £300 are capitalised; computers costing under £300 are charged to general expenses

Required

(a) Find the credit sales figure by preparing the sales ledger control account for the year ended 31 August 20X9.

Sales ledger control account

	£			£
▼		▼		
▼		▼		
▼		▼		

Picklist:

Allowance for doubtful debts
Allowance for doubtful debts adjustment
Balance b/d
Balance c/d
Bank
Bank charges
Cash purchases
Cash sales
Computers at cost
Credit purchases
Credit sales
Drawings
General expenses
Inventory
Irrecoverable debts
Loan

(b) Find the amount of the loan repaid during the year by preparing a summarised bank account for the year ended 31 August 20X9.

Bank account

	£			£
▼			▼	
▼			▼	
▼			▼	
▼			▼	
▼			▼	
▼			▼	

Picklist:

Allowance for doubtful debts
Allowance for doubtful debts adjustment
Balance b/d
Balance c/d
Bank charges
Capital
Cash sales
Computers at cost
Drawings
General expenses
Interest received
Inventory
Irrecoverable debts
Loan
Purchases ledger control account
Sales ledger control account

BPP
LEARNING MEDIA

4 Deriving missing figures using a cost structure

Where inventory, sales or purchases is the unknown figure, one method of calculating the missing figure is to use a **cost structure**.

The cost structure is usually expressed in one of two ways, as either a margin or a mark-up.

Formulae to learn

(a) **Margin**: Here gross profit is expressed as a percentage of sales. For example, a margin of 25% gives:

Sales	100%
Cost of goods sold	75%
Gross profit	25%

(b) **Mark-up**: Here gross profit is expressed as a percentage of cost of goods sold. For example, a mark-up of 35% gives:

Sales	135%
Cost of goods sold	100%
Gross profit	35%

The formulae will be explained through illustrations.

Illustration 2: Using margin to calculate a missing figure

For the year ended 31 December 20X1, a business makes sales of £160,000. The profit margin is 40% of sales.

What is the cost of goods sold for the year ended 31 December 20X1?

Approach

Cost of goods sold can be derived from the value of sales as follows.

	%	£
Sales (a margin, therefore sales is 100%)	100	160,000
Cost of goods sold (balancing %)	60	96,000
Gross profit (% per scenario)	40	64,000

Solution

£	96,000

Workings

160,000/100 × 60 = 96,000

Illustration 3: Using mark-up to calculate a missing figure

For the year ended 31 December 20X2, a business has cost of goods sold of £260,000. The business has a mark-up on cost of 30%.

What are sales for the year ended 31 December 20X2?

Approach

Sales can be derived from the cost of goods sold as follows.

	%	£
Sales (gross profit % plus 100%)	130	338,000
Cost of goods sold (a mark-up, therefore cost of goods sold is 100%)	100	260,000
Gross profit (% per scenario)	30	78,000

Solution

£	338,000

Workings

260,000/100 × 130 = 338,000

BPP
LEARNING MEDIA

As we saw in Level 3 *Advanced Bookkeeping,* in the statement of profit or loss, cost of goods sold is calculated as follows:

Cost of goods sold

	£	£
Opening inventory	X	
Purchases	X	
Closing inventory	(X)	
Cost of goods sold		X

Activity 5: Using margins to calculate missing balances

W Co has on average a profit margin of 40%. In 20X9, sales totalled £476,000.

What is the cost of goods sold?

£	

Workings

Activity 6: Using mark-ups to calculate missing balances

Y Co operates with a standard mark-up of 30% and has the following information available for 20X9.

	£
Sales	221,000
Opening inventories	43,000
Closing inventories	47,500

What is the value for purchases in 20X9?

£ _____

Workings

BPP
LEARNING MEDIA

5 The accounting equation

The accounting equation and statement of financial position were introduced in your Level 2 accounting studies. The statement of financial position will be studied in more detail in Chapter 3 *Accounts for Sole Traders.*

In the context of **incomplete records**, it is useful to see the relationship between the accounting equation and the statement of financial position. The accounting equation can be used to derive missing financial information.

The accounting equation is often stated as:

Assets – Liabilities = Capital

Illustration 4 demonstrates how the statement of financial position for Stockton Trading may be expressed in terms of the accounting equation.

Illustration 4: The accounting equation and the statement of financial position

Stockton Trading
Statement of financial position as at 31 December 20X9

	Cost £	Accumulated depreciation £	Carrying amount £
Non-current assets			
Land and buildings	160,000	60,000	100,000
Office equipment	70,000	20,000	50,000
Motor vehicles	58,000	8,000	50,000
	288,000	88,000	200,000
Current assets			
Inventory	50,000		
Trade receivables	14,000		
Prepayments	3,000		
Cash and cash equivalents	7,000		
		74,000	
Current liabilities			
Trade payables	40,000		
Accruals	4,000		

	Cost £	Accumulated depreciation £	Carrying amount £
		44,000	
Net current assets			30,000
Non-current liabilities			
Bank loans			40,000
Net assets			190,000
Financed by:			
Capital			
Opening capital			170,000
Add: Profit for the year			45,000
Less: Drawings			(25,000)
Closing capital			190,000

Explanation

The statement of financial position for Stockton Trading shows total assets of £274,000 (non-current assets of £200,000 plus current assets of £74,000).

Total liabilities are £84,000 (non-current liabilities of £40,000 plus current liabilities of £44,000).

This is financed by capital of £190,000.

The accounting equation expresses the statement of financial position as an equation, as the top section should come to the same total as the lower section.

You can see from the statement of financial position that:

Assets   –   Liabilities   =   Capital

£274,000   –   £84,000   =   £190,000

Assessment focus point

The accounting equation is very important. In the exam you may be asked to show whether it is correctly stated in a scenario or to use it to calculate a missing figure.

BPP
LEARNING MEDIA

The equation can be rearranged. For example:

Assets = Liabilities + Capital

Assets – Capital = Liabilities

Activity 7: The accounting equation

At 31 January 20X4, the assets and liabilities of a business were as follows:

	£
Plant and machinery	10,000
Motor vehicles	5,000
Capital	20,500
Trade payables	3,000
Trade receivables	2,000
Drawings	1,600
Inventories	4,500
Accruals	250
Bank (debit)	3,500
Cash	250
Profit for the period	3,100

Required

Complete the accounting equation at 31 January 20X4.

Assets = £	Capital £	+ Profit – £	Drawings £	+ Liabilities £

Activity 8: Missing balances and the accounting equation

This task is about calculating missing balances and the accounting equation.

You are given the following information about a sole trader as at 1 September 20X8:

- A sole trader started a business.

- The business was not registered for VAT.

- The sole trader transferred £15,000 of her own money into the business bank account.

- £600 was paid from this account for some computers.

- Goods for resale by the business costing £1,400 were purchased using the trader's personal bank account.

Required

(a) Calculate the capital account as at 1 September 20X8, showing clearly the balance carried down.

Capital account

	£			£
▼		Balance b/d		0
▼			▼	
▼			▼	

Picklist:

Balance b/d
Balance c/d
Bank
Computers at cost
Drawings
Purchases
Purchases ledger control account
Sales
Sales ledger control account
Suspense

BPP
LEARNING MEDIA

The following day, the trader made her first cash sale. A profit was made on the sale. The receipt was banked and the transaction entered in the records.

(b) **Tick the appropriate boxes to show how this transaction affects the elements of the accounting equation below.**

You must choose ONE answer for EACH row.

	Increase ✓	Decrease ✓	No change ✓
Assets			
Liabilities			
Capital			

You are given the following information about another sole trader:

- The cash book shows a debit balance of £4,250.

- The bank statement on the same date shows that the business has a credit balance of £7,500.

(c) **Which ONE of the following could explain this difference?**

	✓
Direct debits on the bank statement have not been entered in the cash book.	
Cheques to suppliers sent out at the end of the month have not yet cleared.	
A receipt from a trade receivable has been posted to the bank account in the general ledger twice.	

6 Goods drawn by proprietor

Often owners will withdraw cash from the business for their own personal use. This needs to be recorded in the accounting records and is entered via the journal:

Account name	Debit £	Credit £
Drawings (SOFP)	X	
Cash (SOFP)		X

Owners may also take goods for their own use from the business. These are also **drawings** but are recorded as follows:

Account name	Debit £	Credit £
Drawings (SOFP)	X	
Purchases (SPL)		X

Drawings of goods are recorded at the **cost** to the business and not at their sales value.

They are taken out of purchases and **not** recorded against inventories.

In incomplete records questions, you must ensure that all drawings are included, whether they are in the form of cash or goods.

Illustration 5: Drawings of goods

During the year ended 31 December 20X9, Peter Albert, a sole trader, carried out the following transactions:

	£
Sales (40 units @ £100)	4,000
Purchases (45 units @ £60)	2,700
His inventory (at cost) was:	
1 January 20X9 (5 units @ £60)	300
31 December 20X9 (8 units @ £60)	480

During the year, he had withdrawn two units for his own use.

First, ignoring the drawings, an outline trading account would appear as follows:

BPP LEARNING MEDIA

	£	£
Sales		4,000
Cost of goods sold		
Opening inventory	300	
Purchases	2,700	
	3,000	
Less closing inventory	(480)	
		2,520
Gross profit		1,480

How should the drawings of goods be treated?

The debit entry will be to drawings on the statement of financial position, but what about the credit entry?

It will **not** go to inventory (because these goods were not in hand at the year end and so they are not included in the value of £480) but rather the adjustment will go to the **purchases account** (as this is where they will have been previously recorded).

In the trading account, this credit entry is often shown as a separate deduction from cost of goods sold. For example:

	£	£
Sales		4,000
Cost of goods sold		
Opening inventory	300	
Purchases	2,700	
Less goods drawn by proprietor (2 units @ £60)	(120)	
	2,880	
Less closing inventory	(480)	
		2,400
Gross profit		1,600

Points to note

1 Drawings of goods are recorded at cost.

2 The gross profit figure now makes sense, ie profit of £40 per unit × 40 units sold.

Activity 9: Calculating missing balances and the preparation of final accounts

This task is about calculating missing balances and the preparation of final accounts.

You have the following information about a sole trader:

Assets and liabilities as at 1 May 20X4	£
Plant at carrying amount	71,500
Inventory	10,000
Bank (debit balance on bank statement)	3,200
Trade payables	16,100

There were no other assets or liabilities.

Required

(a) Calculate the following as at 1 May 20X4. Do not enter any figure as negative.

Assets	£	
Liabilities	£	
Capital	£	

During the year ended 30 April 20X5, sales of £47,450 were made. The trader operates with a mark-up of 30%.

(b) Calculate the cost of goods sold for the year ended 30 April 20X5.

£

Purchases for the year were £48,500.

(c) Calculate the value of closing inventory.

£

BPP
LEARNING MEDIA

The trader now tells you that during the year he has taken some goods for personal use.

(d) Complete the following statement:

This means that the inventory figures in the final accounts at 30 April 20X5 will be	
▼	the figure calculated in (c) above.

Picklist:

greater than
less than
the same as

(e) Which of the following is best described as a current asset? Choose ONE answer.

	✓
A bank overdraft	
Drawings that the owner has taken during the year	
Monies owed from a credit customer	
Monies owed to a credit supplier	

Chapter summary

- Some businesses do not keep records of all financial transactions. However, this information is still needed to prepare final accounts.

- There are several techniques which can be used to derive missing numbers from incomplete financial information.

- General ledger accounts can be used to derive missing numbers, including the sales ledger control account, the purchases ledger control account, the bank account and the VAT account.

- Mark-ups and margins can also be used to calculate missing numbers. A cost structure must be set up and appropriate percentages applied.

- The accounting equation demonstrates that the assets less the liabilities of a business are always equal to the capital. The accounting equation can also be used to derive missing financial information.

BPP
LEARNING MEDIA

Keywords

- **Cost structure:** The relationship in percentage terms between sales, cost of goods sold and gross profit

- **Drawings:** Assets taken out of the business by its owner in the form of cash or other items, such as inventory

- **Incomplete records:** Accounting records which are not a full set of primary records and general ledger accounts

- **Margin:** Gross profit expressed as a percentage of sales

- **Mark-up:** The percentage added to cost of goods sold so as to arrive at the selling price

1   A business has an opening balance on the sales ledger control account of £6,700 and a closing balance on the sales ledger control account of £3,200. Credit sales for the period are £69,400.

What was the amount received from credit customers during the period?

£ [   ]

2   A business sells its goods at a mark-up of 45% on cost. The sales for the year were £184,150.

What was the cost of goods sold for the year?

£ [   ]

3   A business operates with a margin of 35%. The cost of goods sold during the year was £130,000.

What were the sales for the year?

£ [   ]

4   A business has made a profit for the year of £17,800. The opening net assets were £58,900 and the closing net assets were £71,400. The owner had paid an additional £10,000 of capital into the business during the year.

What were the drawings during the year?

£ [   ]

5   A business had a positive balance in the bank general ledger account at the start and end of the year. The opening balance was £1,020 and the closing balance £890.

During the year, takings of £48,700 were paid into the bank account and expenses of £37,100 were paid from the bank account.

Records of the owner's drawings had not been maintained.

What were the owner's drawings for the year?

£ [   ]

BPP
LEARNING MEDIA

Accounts for sole traders

3

Learning outcomes

4.1	**Calculate opening and/or closing capital for a sole trader**
	• Account for drawings, capital injections and profits or losses
	• Record these in ledger accounts
	• Explain movements in capital balances
4.2	**Describe the components of a set of final accounts for a sole trader**
	• The purpose of a statement of profit or loss
	• The purpose of a statement of financial position
	• How the statement of financial position is linked to the accounting equation
	• How the statement of profit or loss and the statement of financial position are related
4.3	**Prepare a statement of profit or loss for a sole trader in the given format**
	• Itemise income and expenditure in line with given organisational policies
	• Transfer data from the trial balance to the appropriate line of the statement according to the level of detail given for the organisation
4.4	**Prepare a statement of financial position for a sole trader in the given format**
	• Apply the net assets presentation of the statement of financial position
	• Transfer data from the trial balance to the appropriate line of the statement according to the level of detail given for the organisation

Assessment context

Questions on this chapter will be tested in Task 3 of the exam. This task is likely to present you with an adjusted trial balance (which balances) and you will be required to draw up a statement of profit or loss and/or a statement of financial position using the skeleton proformas provided.

Qualification context

This area completes your studies in relation to producing the final accounts for a sole trader. The concepts and principles, however, are further developed in the next chapter on partnerships, and in the preparation of the financial statements of limited companies which is examined in the Level 4 paper *Financial Statements of Limited Companies*.

Business context

All businesses need to produce financial information so that the owners know how the business has performed over a period of time. For many, this will involve the production of the statement of profit or loss and statement of financial position. The statement of profit or loss is also often used by a business to prepare information for the tax authorities.

BPP LEARNING MEDIA

Chapter overview

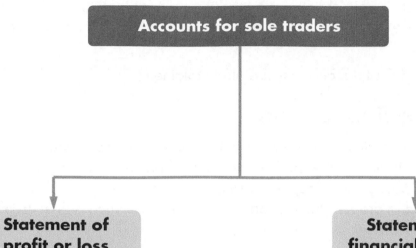

Accounts for sole traders

Statement of profit or loss

Shows the income and expenses of the business for a period of time

Statement of financial position

Shows the assets, liabilities and capital of the business at a point in time

Introduction

In the Level 3 *Advanced Bookkeeping* unit we saw how a trial balance is prepared at the period end. In this chapter, we take this a stage further by using the trial balance to produce final accounts: a statement of profit or loss and a statement of financial position.

The components of the final accounts are also explained.

1 Preparing final accounts

As we have seen in earlier studies, financial transactions are recorded in the books of prime entry. Periodically, the totals of the books of prime entry are posted to the general ledger. At the period end, the closing balances on the general ledger accounts are used to prepare the trial balance. The trial balance is then used to produce the final accounts.

The recommended steps to follow when preparing final accounts are as follows:

Step 1: Review the trial balance.

Step 2: Identify the items on the trial balance which should be transferred to the statement of profit or loss. Record these items in the statement of profit or loss proforma.

Step 3: Cast (add down) the statement of profit or loss, including totals where appropriate.

Step 4: Note the figure for profit/(loss) for the year. This will later be transferred to the statement of financial position.

Step 5: Identify the items on the trial balance which should be transferred to the statement of financial position. Record these items in the statement of financial position proforma.

Step 6: Enter the profit or loss figure calculated in the statement of profit or loss in the capital section of the statement of financial position.

Step 7: Cast the statement of financial position, including totals where appropriate.

Step 8: Review the completed proformas. If you have entered the items correctly, the statement of financial position will balance.

BPP
LEARNING MEDIA

Assessment focus point

When you are preparing final accounts in the assessment, items must be entered under the correct main heading and with the right numerical entry on the corresponding row.

However, items may be entered in any order under that heading.

For example, under current assets, inventory, trade receivables and cash can be entered in any order. As long as they are all entered under current assets and matched with the correct amounts, full marks will be awarded for this section of the statement of financial position.

The components of the final accounts and the process of preparing a statement of profit or loss and a statement of financial position from a trial balance will be explained through Illustrations 1 and 2.

Information for use in Illustrations 1 and 2

This task is about preparing final accounts for sole traders.

You have the following trial balance for a sole trader known as Stockton Trading. All the necessary year-end adjustments have been made.

Stockton Trading

Trial balance for the year ended 31 July 20X4

	Debit £	Credit £
Accruals		4,000
Bank loan		40,000
Capital		170,000
Carriage inwards	20,000	
Carriage outwards	4,000	
Cash	7,000	
Closing inventory	50,000	50,000
Depreciation charges	7,000	
Discounts allowed	1,000	
Discounts received		3,000
Drawings	25,000	
Electricity	2,000	

	Debit £	Credit £
Interest received		5,000
Land and buildings at cost	160,000	
Land and buildings accumulated depreciation		60,000
Motor vehicles at cost	58,000	
Motor vehicles accumulated depreciation		8,000
Office equipment at cost	70,000	
Office equipment accumulated depreciation		20,000
Opening inventory	40,000	
Prepayments	3,000	
Purchases	110,000	
Purchases ledger control account		40,000
Rent	17,000	
Sales		200,000
Sales ledger control account	14,000	
Wages and salaries	12,000	
Total	**600,000**	**600,000**

Required

Illustration 1:

Prepare a statement of profit or loss for Stockton Trading for the year ended 31 July 20X4.

If necessary, use a minus sign to indicate ONLY the following:

- **The deduction of an account balance used to make up cost of goods sold**

- **A loss for the year**

Illustration 2:

Prepare a statement of financial position for Stockton Trading for the year ended 31 July 20X4. If necessary, use a minus sign to indicate drawings.

BPP
LEARNING MEDIA

1.1 Statement of profit or loss

The **statement of profit or loss** provides a summary of the income and expenses incurred by the business over a period of time (usually 12 months).

It shows the income earned by the business (revenue) and the costs the business has incurred (expenses). Income less expenses gives the profit the business has generated.

The following are examples of income:

(a) Revenue (or sales) – this is all the income generated from selling the business's primary product

(b) Interest received – eg interest received from bank savings accounts

(c) Rental income

The following are examples of expenses:

(a) Cost of goods sold – this is the cost to the business of the products that it sells
(b) Interest charges – eg interest charged on bank loans
(c) Gas, electricity, stationery and rent costs

Illustration 1: Preparing a statement of profit or loss from a trial balance

Step 1: Review the trial balance.

Step 2: Identify the items on the trial balance which should be transferred to the statement of profit or loss. Record these items in the statement of profit or loss proforma.

In this illustration these items are as follows:

Stockton Trading
Trial balance for the year ended 31 July 20X4 – extract

	Debit £	Credit £
Carriage inwards	20,000	
Carriage outwards	4,000	
Closing inventory		50,000
Depreciation charges	7,000	
Discounts allowed	1,000	
Discounts received		3,000
Electricity	2,000	
Interest received		5,000
Opening inventory	40,000	
Purchases	110,000	
Rent	17,000	
Sales		200,000
Wages and salaries	12,000	

Step 3: Cast (add down) the statement of profit or loss, including totals where appropriate.

Step 4: Note the figure for profit/(loss) for the year. This will later be transferred to the statement of financial position.

BPP LEARNING MEDIA

Solution

Stockton Trading
Statement of profit or loss for the year ended 31 July 20X4

	£	£
Sales revenue		200,000
Opening inventory	40,000	
Purchases	110,000	
Carriage inwards	20,000	
Closing inventory	(50,000)	
Cost of goods sold		120,000
Gross profit		80,000
Add:		
Interest received		5,000
Discounts received		3,000
Less:		
Carriage outwards	4,000	
Depreciation charges	7,000	
Discounts allowed	1,000	
Electricity	2,000	
Rent	17,000	
Wages and salaries	12,000	
Total expenses		43,000
Profit for the year		45,000

In the statement of profit and loss, a profit for the year figure of £45,000 has been calculated. This will be transferred to the capital section of the statement of financial position in Illustration 2.

CENTRAL BEDS COLLEGE LIBRARY

1.1.1 Points to note

Cost of goods sold is calculated as the following:

- **Opening inventory** (all the goods the business purchased in the last period but did not sell)
- Plus **purchases** (all the goods the business has bought to sell in this period)
- **Carriage inwards** (this is part of the cost of acquiring the goods)
- Less **closing inventory** (all the goods the business has bought in this period but not yet sold)

Gross profit is the profit from the business's trading activity.

Discounts received are prompt payment discounts the business has received from suppliers.

The expenses are the business's overheads.

The **profit for the year** is then transferred to the **capital** section of the **statement of financial position**.

Assessment focus point

In the assessment, accounts such as discounts received and interest received should be treated as separate additions to gross profit, rather than shown as a 'negative expense'.

The proformas will be set out in a format which enables you to position these items correctly.

1.2 Statement of financial position

The statement of financial position is a snapshot of the business at a single point in time.

The top section shows what a business owns (**assets**) and what it owes (**liabilities**). Assets are shown as **non-current assets** or **current assets**, and liabilities are shown as **non-current liabilities** or **current liabilities**.

It is important to understand the 'capital section' of a sole trader's statement of financial position. An existing business will have an opening balance at the start of the year. This is the money that has accumulated over previous years and is owed to the owner.

Any further capital that the owner contributes to the business will increase the amount due to the owner.

During the course of the current year, the capital owed to the owner will increase by any profit generated by the business, or will decrease if a loss arises.

The owner may well withdraw money from the business for personal use. Money or goods that the owner takes out of the business are known as 'drawings'. Drawings decrease the owner's investment in the business. They are not regarded as a

BPP
LEARNING MEDIA

business expense and therefore are deducted from the capital section of the statement of financial position rather than being included in the statement of profit or loss.

Illustration 2: Preparing a statement of financial position from a trial balance

Step 5: Identify the items on the trial balance which should be transferred to the statement of financial position. Record these items in the statement of financial position proforma.

In this illustration these items are as follows:

Stockton Trading
Trial balance for the year ended 31 July 20X4

	Debit £	Credit £
Accruals		4,000
Bank loan		40,000
Capital		170,000
Cash	7,000	
Closing inventory	50,000	
Drawings	25,000	
Land and buildings at cost	160,000	
Land and buildings accumulated depreciation		60,000
Motor vehicles at cost	58,000	
Motor vehicles accumulated depreciation		8,000
Office equipment at cost	70,000	
Office equipment accumulated depreciation		20,000
Prepayments	3,000	
Purchases ledger control account		40,000
Sales ledger control account	14,000	

Step 6: Enter the profit or loss figure calculated in the statement of profit or loss in the capital section of the statement of financial position.

Step 7: Cast the statement of financial position, including totals where appropriate.

Step 8: Review the completed proformas. If you have entered the items correctly, the statement of financial position will balance.

Stockton Trading
Statement of financial position as at 31 July 20X4

	Cost £	Accumulated depreciation £	Carrying amount £
Non-current assets			
Land and buildings	160,000	60,000	100,000
Office equipment	70,000	20,000	50,000
Motor vehicles	58,000	8,000	50,000
	288,000	88,000	200,000
Current assets			
Inventory	50,000		
Trade receivables	14,000		
Prepayments	3,000		
Cash and cash equivalents	7,000		
		74,000	
Current liabilities			
Trade payables	40,000		
Accruals	4,000		
		44,000	
Net current assets			30,000
Non-current liabilities			
Bank loans			40,000
Net assets			190,000
Financed by:			
Opening capital			170,000
Add: Profit for the year			45,000
Less: Drawings			(25,000)
Closing capital			190,000

BPP
LEARNING MEDIA

1.2.1 Useful terms

Term	Consideration
Accounting equation	The statement of financial position falls naturally into two main sections, and it is these sections which are the two sides of the accounting equation – 'assets minus liabilities' and 'capital'.
	(Under International Accounting Standards the statement of financial position can be presented in a different format, with assets in the top section and capital plus liabilities in the lower section.)
Non-current assets	These are assets held and used in the business over the long term (ie for more than one year).
	Property, plant and equipment are often a significant component of non-current assets. These are assets which have a physical substance, for example buildings, motor vehicles and machinery.
Current assets	These are assets which the business will hold for less than one year and are often used by the business for day-to-day trading. Current assets include inventories, trade receivables and bank/cash balances.
Current liabilities	These are liabilities owed by the business which will be settled in less than one year. They often arise from day-to-day activities and include trade payables, accruals and bank overdrafts.
	Where a business is registered for VAT, it acts as a collecting agent for the Government. The balance on the VAT control account is often a current liability because businesses tend to sell items for more than they cost, and so the VAT owed on sales will be higher than the VAT due back on purchases.
Net current assets	This is the total of the current assets minus the current liabilities.
Non-current liabilities	These are the long-term debts of the business and include items such as long-term bank loans.
Net assets	Non-current liabilities are deducted from non-current assets and net current assets to give a total for the top section of the statement of financial position.
	In terms of the accounting equation, this is the total of the assets minus liabilities.
Capital	The capital section of the statement of financial position shows the amount the business owes back to its owner. This includes the capital contributed to date, plus the profits for the year, less any drawings taken.
	It is also known as the proprietor's interest.

1.3 Assessment tasks

Assessment focus point

Assessment tasks on this topic will ask you to prepare a statement of profit or loss and/or a statement of financial position from the adjusted balances on a trial balance. A proforma will be provided with drop down boxes for narrative entries and gap fill spaces for numerical entries.

Tasks may also test your understanding of the components of the final accounts.

The activity below gives you the opportunity to practise the skills you will need in the assessment.

Activity 1: Preparing final accounts for a sole trader

This task is about preparing final accounts for sole traders.

You have the following trial balance for a sole trader known as Pearl Trading. All the necessary year-end adjustments have been made.

The following are accounting policies used by Pearl Trading:

- Sales revenue should include sales returns, if any.
- Purchases should include purchases returns and carriage inwards, if any.

Required

(a) **Calculate the sales revenue figure to be included in the statement of profit or loss for Pearl Trading.**

£

(b) **Calculate the purchases figure to be included in the statement of profit or loss for Pearl Trading.**

£

(c) **Prepare a statement of profit or loss for Pearl Trading for the year ended 31 August 20X9.**

If necessary, use a minus sign to indicate ONLY the following:

- **The deduction of an account balance used to make up cost of goods sold**

- **A loss for the year**

BPP
LEARNING MEDIA

Pearl Trading

Trial balance for the year ended 31 August 20X9

	Debit £	Credit £
Accruals		5,310
Bank	5,034	
Capital		20,000
Carriage inwards	4,345	
Carriage outwards	6,421	
Closing inventory	26,424	26,424
Depreciation charges	9,524	
Disposal of non-current asset		510
Drawings	16,000	
General expenses	9,521	
Machinery at cost	20,000	
Machinery accumulated depreciation		8,321
Opening inventory	18,311	
Prepayments	780	
Purchases	180,130	
Purchases ledger control account		30,300
Sales		270,314
Sales ledger control account	38,310	
Sales returns	9,020	
VAT		22,952
Wages	40,311	
Total	**384,131**	**384,131**

Pearl Trading

Statement of profit or loss for the year ended 31 August 20X9

	£	£
Sales revenue		
▼		
▼		
▼		
▼		
Cost of goods sold		
Gross profit		
Add:		
▼		
Less:		
▼		
▼		
▼		
▼		
Total expenses		
Profit/loss for the year		

Picklist:

Accruals
Add: Profit for the year
Capital
Carriage outwards
Cash and cash equivalents
Closing inventory
Depreciation charges
Disposal of non-current asset
General expenses
Less: Drawings
Less: Loss for the year
Machinery
Opening inventory
Prepayments
Purchases
Sales

BPP
LEARNING MEDIA

Trade payables
Trade receivables
VAT
Wages

(d) Prepare a statement of financial position for Pearl Trading for the year ended 31 August 20X9. If necessary, use a minus sign to indicate drawings.

Pearl Trading

Statement of financial position as at 31 August 20X9

	Cost £	Accumulated depreciation £	Carrying amount £
Non-current assets			
▼			
Current assets			
▼			
▼			
▼			
▼			
▼			

	Cost £	Accumulated depreciation £	Carrying amount £
Current liabilities			
▼			
▼			
▼			
▼			
Net current assets			
Net assets			
Financed by:			
Capital			
Opening capital			
▼			
▼			
Closing capital			

Picklist:

Accruals
Add: Profit for the year
Capital
Carriage outwards
Cash and cash equivalents
Depreciation charges
Disposal of non-current asset
General expenses
Inventory
Less: Drawings
Less: Loss for the year
Machinery
Prepayments
Purchases
Sales
Trade payables
Trade receivables

BPP
LEARNING MEDIA

VAT
Wages

(e) Identify ONE valid reason for producing an initial trial balance.

	✓
It shows whether the business has made a profit or a loss for the period.	
It proves that double entry has taken place.	
It shows which items belong in the statement of profit or loss and statement of financial position.	
It is produced automatically by a computerised accounting system.	

You are preparing the final accounts for an organisation when you notice the following inconsistency in the books and records:

- The cost of computers in the initial trial balance shows a debit balance of £41,000.

- The total cost of the computers from a list of those present at the year end was £55,000.

(f) Which ONE of the following could explain this difference?

	✓
A newly purchased computer was not included in the physical count.	
The theft of a computer has not been recorded in the non-current assets register.	
The sale of a computer has been omitted from the initial trial balance.	
The purchase of a computer has not been posted to the general ledger.	

2 Cost of goods sold and inventory in the trial balance

In the example above, the components of cost of goods sold and inventory were presented on several lines of the trial balance. Therefore, the trial balance identifies:

- Opening inventory
- Purchases
- Carriage inwards
- Closing inventory

Closing inventory is shown on the debit side (being an asset in the statement of financial position at the year end) and also on the credit side (being a reduction in cost of goods sold transferred to the statement of profit or loss at the end of the period).

All other cost of goods sold items are debit balances because they form part of the expense transferred to the statement of profit or loss at the end of the period.

2.1 Alternative presentation of cost of goods sold and inventory

You may also see cost of goods sold and inventory shown on two lines in the trial balance. Under this presentation they would appear as follows:

Pearl Trading
Trial balance for the year ended 31 August 20X9

	Debit £	Credit £
Closing inventory	26,424	
Cost of goods sold	176,362	

Here, the statement of profit or loss balances (opening inventory, purchases, carriage inwards and closing inventory) have been totalled and shown on the cost of goods sold line.

Closing inventory is shown on a separate line and represents the asset listed in the statement of financial position at the year end.

An example of this alternative presentation will be studied further in Chapter 4 *Accounts for Partnerships*.

BPP
LEARNING MEDIA

Chapter summary

- At the period end, the closing balances on the general ledger accounts are used to prepare the trial balance. The trial balance is then used to prepare the final accounts.

- The recommended steps to follow when preparing final accounts are as follows:

  Step 1: Review the trial balance.

  Step 2: Identify the items on the trial balance which should be transferred to the statement of profit or loss. Record these items in the statement of profit or loss proforma.

  Step 3: Cast (add down) the statement of profit or loss, including totals where appropriate.

  Step 4: Note the figure for profit/(loss) for the year. This will later be transferred to the statement of financial position.

  Step 5: Identify the items on the trial balance which should be transferred to the statement of financial position. Record these items in the statement of financial position proforma.

  Step 6: Enter the profit or loss figure calculated in the statement of profit or loss in the capital section of the statement of financial position.

  Step 7: Cast the statement of financial position, including totals where appropriate.

  Step 8: Review the completed proformas. If you have entered the items correctly, the statement of financial position will balance.

- **Capital:** The capital or proprietor's interest section of the statement of financial position shows the amount the business owes to its owner

- **Current assets:** These are assets which the business will hold for less than one year and are often used by the business for day-to-day trading

- **Current liabilities:** These are liabilities owed by the business which will be settled in less than one year

- **Gross profit:** This is the profit earned by the business from its trading activities

- **Net assets:** These are total assets less total liabilities

- **Net current assets:** These are the total of the current assets minus the current liabilities

- **Non-current assets:** These are assets held and used in the business over the long term (ie more than one year)

- **Non-current liabilities:** These are liabilities that are due to be paid more than a year after the statement of financial position date

- **Profit for the year:** This is the profit earned by the business after all expenses have been deducted

- **Statement of financial position:** This statement lists all of the assets, liabilities and capital of the business on the year-end date of the accounting period

- **Statement of profit or loss:** The statement of profit or loss provides a summary of the income and expenses incurred by the business over a period of time (usually 12 months)

BPP
LEARNING MEDIA

Test your learning

1 **Which TWO of the following are examples of current assets?**

	✓
Inventories	
Trade payables	
Trade receivables	
Profit	

2 A business has non-current assets of £20,000, trade receivables of £2,000, a positive bank balance of £4,000, trade payables of £3,000 and a non-current bank loan of £10,000.

According to the accounting equation, what is capital?

	✓
£29,000	
£13,000	
£16,000	
£42,000	

3 **Is the following statement true or false?**

Drawings are an expense of the business.

	✓
True	
False	

4   A sole trader has the following balances in her initial trial balance at
31 May 20X8:

	£
Furniture and fittings at cost	12,600
Motor vehicles at cost	38,500
Accumulated depreciation at 1 June 20X7:	
Furniture and fittings	3,400
Motor vehicles	15,500

Furniture and fittings are depreciated at the rate of 20% per annum on cost, and motor vehicles are depreciated on the diminishing balance basis at a rate of 30%.

Complete the table below to show the total carrying amount of the non-current assets that will appear in the statement of financial position at 31 May 20X8.

Non-current assets

	Cost £	Accumulated depreciation £	Carrying amount £
Furniture and fittings			
Motor vehicles			

BPP
LEARNING MEDIA

5   This task is about preparing final accounts for sole traders.

You have the following trial balance for a sole trader known as Bernard Trading. All the necessary year-end adjustments have been made.

Bernard Trading
Trial balance for the year ended 31 December 20X7

	Debit £	Credit £
Accruals		600
Bank overdraft		13,300
Capital		60,000
Carriage outwards	4,100	
Closing inventory	18,000	18,000
Depreciation charges	24,000	
Drawings	20,000	
Loan interest	800	
Machinery at cost	73,000	
Machinery accumulated depreciation		30,000
Miscellaneous expenses	2,000	
Opening inventory	16,500	
Office costs	2,400	
Prepayments	400	
Purchases	196,000	
Purchases ledger control account		32,100
Sales		258,000
Sales ledger control account	64,600	
Telephone expenses	2,200	
VAT due to HMRC		12,000
Total	**424,000**	**424,000**

The following are accounting policies used by Bernard Trading:

- Sales revenue should include sales returns, if any.
- Purchases should include purchases returns and carriage inwards, if any.

(a) **Prepare a statement of profit or loss for Bernard Trading for the year ended 31 December 20X7.**

If necessary, use a minus sign to indicate ONLY the following:

- **The deduction of an account balance used to make up cost of goods sold**

- **A loss for the year**

Bernard Trading

Statement of profit or loss for the year ended 31 December 20X7

	£	£
Sales revenue		
▼		
▼		
▼		
▼		
Cost of goods sold		
Gross profit		
Less:		
▼		
▼		
▼		
▼		
▼		
▼		
Total expenses		
Profit/loss for the year		

Picklist:

Accruals
Add: Profit for the year
Bank overdraft
Capital
Carriage outwards

BPP
LEARNING MEDIA

Closing inventory
Depreciation charges
Less: Drawings
Less: Loss for the year
Loan interest
Machinery
Miscellaneous expenses
Office costs
Opening inventory
Prepayments
Purchases
Sales
Telephone expenses
Trade payables
Trade receivables
VAT

(b) Prepare a statement of financial position for Bernard Trading for the year ended 31 December 20X7. If necessary, use a minus sign to indicate drawings.

Bernard Trading
Statement of financial position as at 31 December 20X7

		Cost £	Accumulated depreciation £	Carrying amount £
Non-current assets				
	▼			
Current assets				
	▼			
	▼			
	▼			
	▼			

Current liabilities			
▼			
▼			
▼			
▼			
▼			
Net current assets			
Net assets			
Financed by:			
Capital			
Opening capital			
▼			
▼			
Closing capital			

Picklist:

Accruals
Add: Profit for the year
Bank overdraft
Capital
Carriage outwards
Depreciation charges
Inventory
Less: Drawings
Less: Loss for the year
Loan interest
Machinery
Miscellaneous expenses
Office costs
Prepayments
Purchases
Sales
Telephone expenses
Trade payables
Trade receivables
VAT

BPP
LEARNING MEDIA

Accounts for partnerships

Learning outcomes

5.1	**Describe the key components of a partnership agreement**
	• What a partnership agreement typically may or may not contain
	• Why a formal partnership agreement may not exist for all partnerships
5.2	**Describe the accounting procedures for a change in partners**
	• A simple definition of goodwill in accounting terms
	• Why goodwill will change capital balances on admission or retirement of a partner
	• That goodwill may be introduced and subsequently eliminated from the accounting records using the profit sharing ratio
	• Calculate the goodwill adjustments using the profit sharing ratio
	• Enter such adjustments in ledger accounts and balance off these accounts as necessary
5.3	**Describe the key components of partnership accounts**
	• The purpose of a statement of profit or loss
	• The purpose and content of the partnership appropriation account
	• How the statement of profit or loss is linked to the partnership appropriation account
	• The nature and content of partners' current accounts
	• The nature and content of partners' capital accounts
	• The purpose of a statement of financial position
5.4	**Prepare a statement of profit or loss for a partnership, in the given format**
	• Why the statement of profit or loss for a partnership is an adaptation of one for a sole trader
	• Itemise income and expenditure in line with given organisational policies
	• Transfer data from the trial balance to the appropriate line of the statement according to the level of detail given for the organisation

5.5	**Prepare a partnership appropriation account, in compliance with the partnership agreement and in the given format**
	• Apply the terms of a partnership agreement
	• Record interest on capital (but not how to calculate it)
	• Record interest on drawings (but not how to calculate it)
	• Record salaries or commission paid to partners
	• Calculate, and appropriate and account for, the residual profit according to the profit sharing ratio
	• Recognise the status of partners' salaries, commission and interest
	• Present this account in the format given for the organisation
5.6	**Prepare the current accounts for each partner**
	• Enter ledger accounting entries
	• Account for drawings in the form of cash, goods or services
	• Link the current account with figures from the appropriation account
5.7	**Prepare a statement of financial position for a partnership, in compliance with the partnership agreement and in the given format**
	• How the statement of financial position for a partnership differs from one of a sole trader
	• Apply the net assets presentation of the statement of financial position
	• Transfer data from the trial balance to the appropriate line of the statement according to the level of detail given for the organisation
	• Show partners' current and capital accounts on the statement of financial position

Assessment context

Partnerships will be tested in Tasks 5 and 6 of the assessment. These tasks will require students to calculate the amount to be appropriated to specific partners; prepare partners' current and capital accounts; and prepare an appropriation account and/or a statement of financial position.

Tasks may include the admission of a new partner or the retirement of an existing partner (but not both).

Qualification context

Partnerships are only examined in the *Final Accounts Preparation* unit.

Business context

Partnerships enable two or more individuals to work together with a view to generating profit. Unlike a sole trader, the risks and rewards of ownership are shared. Where two or more people work together, they contribute capital to the organisation and also their experience.

BPP
LEARNING MEDIA

Chapter overview

In a partnership statement of financial position:

- The top section is similar to the statement of financial position for a sole trader
- The financing section is different from the statement of financial position for a sole trader; it comprises partners' current accounts and capital accounts

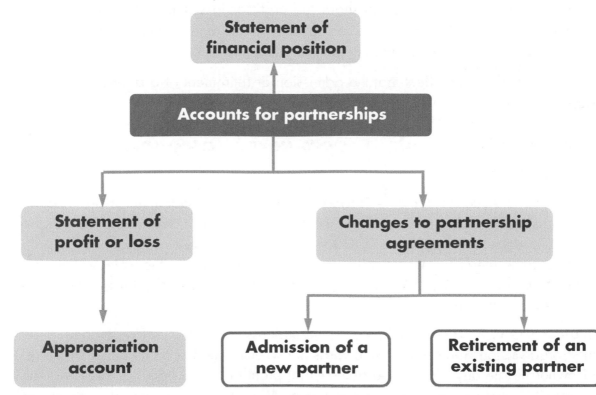

Statement of financial position

Accounts for partnerships

Statement of profit or loss

Changes to partnership agreements

Appropriation account

An account used to share the profit or loss generated by the partnership for a period between the partners according to the partnership agreement

Admission of a new partner

When a partner is admitted:

- They will normally pay capital into the partnership
- This capital will be credited to their capital account and debited to bank/other assets
- The new partnership agreement applies from the date the new partner is admitted into the partnership

Retirement of an existing partner

When a partner retires:

- The final balance on their current account will be transferred to their capital account
- The balance on their capital account will be either paid to them in cash or turned into a partnership loan
- The new partnership agreement applies from the date the new partner retires from the partnership

Introduction

In Chapter 3 *Accounts for Sole Traders* we prepared the final accounts for individuals owning businesses. In this chapter, we develop our knowledge of the accounts preparation process by looking at partnership accounts.

Partnerships are governed by the terms set out in the partnership agreement that is specific to their organisation. The terms have a direct bearing on the accounts.

As partnerships have more than one owner, the final accounts have more components than the accounts for sole traders. For example, a partnership appropriation account is used to share the profit or loss among the partners, and current and capital accounts are used to identify the amount due to each partner. These components will be studied in this chapter.

We also consider the effect that the admission or retirement of a partner has on the accounts.

1 Accounts for sole traders versus accounts for partnerships

In Chapter 3 *Accounts for Sole Traders* we prepared the statement of profit or loss and the statement of financial position for sole traders. The statement of profit or loss is used to calculate the profit or loss for the year. For these organisations, all profit or loss generated by a sole trader's business belongs to the sole trader. The cumulative amount owed to the sole trader is shown in the capital section of the statement of financial position.

In a partnership the owners (partners) of the business work together to manage and run their organisation. They share the rewards of ownership (ie the profit) and also the risk of ownership (ie any losses). The statement of profit or loss is again used to calculate the profit or loss generated by the business each year. However, the profit or loss for the year then needs to be shared among the partners.

Similarly, the cumulative amount owed to the partners is recorded in the financing section of the statement of financial position. However, this amount is shared between the partners and therefore the amount due to each partner is identified in the financing section of the statement of financial position.

The key components of partnership accounts that are not required for sole traders' accounts are:

- Appropriation account
- Current accounts
- Capital accounts
- The financing section of the statement of financial position

These components will be explained through Illustrations 1 to 4.

BPP
LEARNING MEDIA

Assessment focus point

The AAT have confirmed the following in relation to tasks on partnerships:

- All information in a partnership agreement that is relevant to a task will be stated in the scenario.

- The number of partners in a scenario will be limited to a maximum of three.

- There will be a maximum of one change in the partnership at the end of a period (this means there could be either the admission of a new partner or the retirement of an existing partner, but not both).

- Where goodwill arises, it will always be introduced and then subsequently eliminated.

- Limited liability partnerships (LLPs) are not examinable.

- The formation of a partnership from a sole trader will not be tested.

- The dissolution of a partnership will not be tested.

- Interest on drawings and capital will not need to be calculated.

- In longer partnership questions, students will be completing proformas (eg an appropriation account, current accounts, capital accounts, a statement of financial position).

2 Partnership agreements

On formation, the partners agree the terms under which the partnership will operate. The terms of the partnership are established through a **partnership agreement**.

A partnership agreement usually covers the following areas:

Area	Consideration
Capital	• This is the amount invested in the business by each individual partner as a source of financing for the partnership. • Partners may contribute the same amount of capital or invest different amounts.
Profit sharing ratio (PSR)	• This ratio is used to share the profits or losses of the business. • It is usually expressed as a percentage of the total profits or losses attributable to each partner. • All partners could have an equal share of the profits or losses, or a higher percentage may be allocated to the more senior partners.

Area	Consideration
Salaries	• Partners may be entitled to a salary. • A salary paid to partners is an appropriation of profit. • It is not an expense in the statement of profit or loss.
Interest on capital	• Partners may be entitled to earn interest on the capital they have contributed to the business. • If interest on capital is paid, an interest rate will be agreed.
Commission paid to partners	• Partners may be entitled to earn commission (eg sales commission). • Commission paid to partners is an appropriation of profit. • It is not an expense in the statement of profit or loss.
Drawings	• Drawings occur when partners withdraw cash or other assets from the organisation for personal use. • The partnership agreement may apply an interest charge on drawings.

A formal partnership agreement is not a requirement for a business relationship to become a partnership. If the partners do not have a formal partnership agreement, the provisions of the Partnership Act 1890 apply.

Assessment focus point

Interest on drawings and interest on capital may need to be recorded in the partnership accounts but they will not need to be calculated. The amount of interest on drawings and/or interest on capital will be stated in the scenario.

We will consider the features of partnership accounts in more detail in the sections which follow.

BPP
LEARNING MEDIA

3 Appropriation account

In the previous chapter we calculated the profit for the year for organisations using a statement of profit or loss proforma.

> **Assessment focus point**
>
> In assessment tasks on partnership accounts, the profit or loss for the period may well be stated in the scenario. This figure can then be used to answer the requirements.
>
> Note that tasks will give clear instructions on whether numbers should be entered as positive figures or whether minus signs should be used.

Once the profit for the period for a partnership has been established, a further proforma is needed to allocate it between partners. The proforma used to allocate the profit or loss for the period among partners is called the **appropriation account**.

When preparing an appropriation account, the steps are as follows:

Step 1: Identify the profit/(loss) for the year (this may well be stated in the scenario). In the appropriation account, enter this on the 'profit/(loss) for appropriation' row.

Step 2: Allocate or charge the following items, where relevant:

- Allocate partners' salaries
- Allocate interest on capital
- Allocate commission earned by partners (eg sales commission)
- Charge interest on drawings

Note. In the appropriation account proforma, these items can be listed in any order. As long as they are matched with the correct amount, full marks will be awarded for this section of the appropriation account.

Step 3: Sum down and calculate the 'Residual profit available for distribution'. Enter this amount in the partnership appropriation account.

Step 4: Allocate the share of residual profit or loss according to the profit sharing ratio.

Step 5: Complete the proforma by entering the 'Total residual profit or loss distributed'. This figure will match the 'Residual profit/(loss) available for distribution'.

Illustration 1: Preparing an appropriation account

This task is about accounting for partnerships. You have the following information about a partnership business:

- The partners are Alex and Ben.
- The financial year ends on 31 December.

Summary of the partnership agreement

	Alex	Ben
Profit share	60%	40%
Annual salaries	£4,000	£1,500
Sales commission for the year	£100	£50
Interest on capital for the year	£600	£450
Interest on drawings for the year	£400	£300
Current account balances at 1 January 20X1	£5,000	£4,000
Capital account balances at 1 January 20X1	£28,000	£17,000
Capital contributions made into the partnership bank account during the year ended 31 December 20X1	£16,000	£14,000
Drawings for the year	£8,000	£6,000

Profit for the year ended 31 December 20X1 was £30,000 before appropriations.

Required

Prepare the appropriation account for the partnership for the year ended 31 December 20X1.

You MUST enter zeros where appropriate in order to obtain full marks.

Use a minus sign for deductions or where there is a loss to be distributed.

BPP
LEARNING MEDIA

Partnership appropriation account for the year ended 31 December 20X1

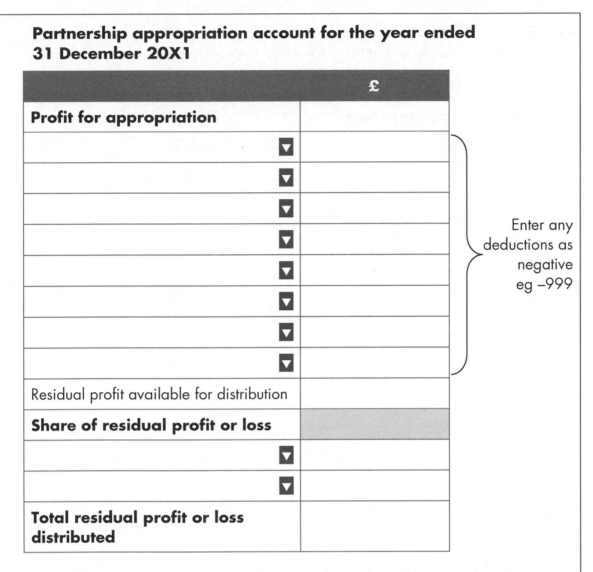

	£
Profit for appropriation	
▼	
▼	
▼	
▼	
▼	
▼	
▼	
▼	
Residual profit available for distribution	
Share of residual profit or loss	
▼	
▼	
Total residual profit or loss distributed	

Enter any deductions as negative eg –999

Step 1: Identify the profit/(loss) for the year (this may well be stated in the scenario). In the appropriation account, enter this on the 'profit/(loss) for appropriation' row.

Partnership appropriation account for the year ended 31 December 20X1

	£
Profit for appropriation	30,000

Step 2: Allocate or charge the following items, where relevant:

- Allocate partners' salaries
- Allocate interest on capital
- Allocate commission earned by partners (eg sales commission)
- Charge interest on drawings

Step 3: Sum down and calculate the 'Residual profit available for distribution'. Enter this amount in the partnership appropriation account.

	£
Profit for appropriation	30,000
Salary – Alex	–4,000
Salary – Ben	–1,500
Sales commission – Alex	–100
Sales commission – Ben	–50
Interest on capital – Alex	–600
Interest on capital – Ben	–450
Interest on drawings – Alex	400
Interest on drawings – Ben	300
Residual profit available for distribution	24,000

Enter any deductions as negative eg –999

Step 4: Allocate the share of residual profit or loss according to the profit sharing ratio.

Step 5: Complete the proforma by entering the 'Total residual profit or loss distributed'. This figure will match the 'Residual profit/(loss) available for distribution'.

Share of residual profit or loss	
Share of profit or loss – Alex (24,000 x 60%)	14,400
Share of profit or loss – Ben (24,000 x 40%)	9,600
Total residual profit or loss distributed	24,000

Explanation

The profit for appropriation of £30,000 has now been allocated to Alex and Ben.

However, at this stage it is not easy to see the total amount that has been appropriated to each partner this period.

BPP
LEARNING MEDIA

4 Current accounts

Partnership **current accounts** are used to record each partner's day-to-day transactions with the business. The main entries in the current account will be the partnership's appropriation of profit for the period. Therefore, this will include:

- Salary
- Commission
- Interest on capital
- Interest on drawings
- Share of profit or loss

Drawings will also be recorded in the current accounts. The balance b/d at the start of the period and the balance c/d at the end of the period will be included too.

Once calculated, the closing balance on the partnership current accounts are recorded in the financing section of the statement of financial position.

When preparing the current accounts for inclusion in the accounting records it is useful to show them as one T-account with an amounts column for each partner on either side of the account.

Note that the partnership current accounts should not be confused with a bank current account. The bank current account is an asset (or liability in the case of an overdraft) which is recorded in the top section of the statement of financial position and has been studied in earlier chapters.

Illustration 2: Preparing partnership current accounts

Illustration 2 uses the same data as Illustration 1. Remember that the share of profit or loss calculated in Illustration 1 is £14,400 for Alex and £9,600 for Ben.

Summary of the partnership agreement

	Alex	Ben
Profit share	60%	40%
Annual salaries	£4,000	£1,500
Sales commission for the year	£100	£50
Interest on capital for the year	£600	£450
Interest on drawings for the year	£400	£300
Current account balances at 1 January 20X1	£5,000	£4,000
Capital account balances at 1 January 20X1	£28,000	£17,000
Capital contributions made into the partnership bank account during the year ended 31 December 20X1	£16,000	£14,000
Drawings for the year	£8,000	£6,000

Required

Complete the current accounts for the partnership for the year ended 31 December 20X1, showing the balances carried down.

Current accounts for the year ended 31 December 20X1

	Alex £	Ben £		Alex £	Ben £
▼			▼		
▼			▼		
▼			▼		
▼			▼		
▼			▼		

BPP
LEARNING MEDIA

Solution

Current accounts for the year ended 31 December 20X1

	Alex £	Ben £		Alex £	Ben £
Drawings	8,000	6,000	Balance b/d	5,000	4,000
Interest on drawings	400	300	Salaries	4,000	1,500
Balance c/d	15,700	9,300	Sales commission	100	50
			Interest on capital	600	450
			Share of profit or loss	14,400	9,600
	24,100	15,600		24,100	15,600

Explanation

The current accounts show that at the end of the year, in respect of day-to-day transactions, £15,700 is due to Alex and £9,300 is due to Ben.

5 Capital accounts

As we have seen, the current accounts are used for partners' day-to-day transactions with the business and will increase and decrease throughout the year. However, the **capital accounts** are used to record the long-term capital that the partners pay into the partnership. The balances in these accounts will remain relatively static.

They will comprise the balance b/d at the start of the period, the balance c/d at the end of the period, and any capital contributions or withdrawals made during the period. Capital contributions usually take the form of a cash injection of funds into the business bank account; however, partners may choose to contribute other assets.

The capital account is shown as one T-account with an amounts column for each partner on either side of the account.

Illustration 3: Preparing partnership capital accounts

Illustration 3 uses the same data as Illustrations 1 and 2. Relevant information for preparing the capital accounts is as follows:

Summary of the partnership agreement

	Alex	Ben
Capital account balances at 1 January 20X1	£28,000	£17,000
Capital contributions made into the partnership bank account during the year ended 31 December 20X1	£16,000	£14,000

Required

Complete the capital accounts for the partnership for the year ended 31 December 20X1, showing the balances carried down.

Capital accounts for the year ended 31 December 20X1

	Alex £	Ben £		Alex £	Ben £
▼			▼		
▼			▼		

Solution

Capital accounts for the year ended 31 December 20X1

	Alex £	Ben £		Alex £	Ben £
Balance c/d	44,000	31,000	Balance b/d	28,000	17,000
			Bank	16,000	14,000
	44,000	31,000		44,000	31,000

Explanation

The capital accounts show that at the end of the year, in respect of long-term financing, £44,000 is due to Alex and £31,000 is due to Ben.

BPP LEARNING MEDIA

6 Financing section in the partnership statement of financial position

Chapter 3 *Accounts for Sole Traders* explained that the capital section of a sole trader's statement of financial position comprises opening capital, profit/(loss), drawings and closing capital. All capital is owed to the sole trader.

However, in partnership accounts the 'financing' section replaces the 'capital' section and shows the amounts owed to individual partners.

Illustration 4: Preparing the financing section of the statement of financial position

Having prepared the current accounts in Illustration 2 and the capital accounts in Illustration 3, we know that at the end of the year the closing balances are as follows:

	Alex	Ben
Capital account balances as at 31 December 20X1	£44,000	£31,000
Current account balances as at 31 December 20X1	£15,700	£9,300

Required

Complete the financing section of the statement of financial position as at 31 December 20X1.

Statement of financial position (extract) for the year ended 31 December 20X1

Financed by	Alex £	Ben £	Total £
▼			
▼			

Solution

Statement of financial position (extract) for the year ended 31 December 20X1

Financed by	Alex £	Ben £	Total £
Capital accounts	44,000	31,000	75,000
Current accounts	15,700	9,300	25,000
	59,700	40,300	100,000

Having been introduced to partnership accounts through Illustrations 1 to 4, this chapter will now focus on the practical application of this information and develop the techniques you need in order to answer questions on this area.

7 Question practice

Activity 1 tests your understanding of key components of partnership accounts – the appropriation account, current accounts, capital accounts and the financing section of the statement of financial position. It is longer than an assessment-standard task and provides useful preparation for the exam style questions which follow.

Activity 1: Callum and Mark

You have the following information about a partnership business for the year ended 31 December 20X8:

- The partners are Callum and Mark.
- The profit of the partnership for the year before appropriations is £50,000.

	Callum	Mark
Profit share	80%	20%
Drawings	£6,000	£8,800
Interest on capital	£800	£400
Annual salaries	Nil	£15,000
Current account balances at 1 January 20X8	£1,000	£2,000
Capital account balances at 1 January 20X8	£10,000	£7,000
Capital contributions into the business bank account	£40,000	£13,000

BPP
LEARNING MEDIA

When completing the following tasks, you must enter zeros where appropriate in order to obtain full marks.

Required

(a) **Prepare the capital accounts for each partner as at 31 December 20X8. Show the balance c/d at the end of the period.**

Capital accounts

	Callum £	Mark £		Callum £	Mark £
▼			▼		
▼			▼		

Picklist:

Balance b/d
Balance c/d
Bank

(b) **Prepare the appropriation account for the partnership business for the year ended 31 December 20X8.**

You MUST enter zeros where appropriate in order to obtain full marks.

Use a minus sign for deductions or where there is a loss to be distributed.

Partnership appropriation account

	£
Profit for appropriation	
Salary – Callum	
Salary – Mark	
Interest on capital – Callum	
Interest on capital – Mark	
Residual profit available for distribution	
Share of residual profit or loss:	
Callum	
Mark	
Total residual profit distributed	

Enter any deductions as negative eg –999

(c) **Prepare the current accounts for each partner as at 31 December 20X8. Show the balance c/d at the end of the period.**

Current accounts

	Callum £	Mark £		Callum £	Mark £
▼			▼		
▼			▼		
▼			▼		
▼			▼		

Picklist:

Balance b/d
Balance c/d
Drawings
Interest on capital
Salaries
Share of profit or loss

(d) **Show the partners' capital and current account balances in the statement of financial position. Enter the net assets figure.**

Callum and Mark
Statement of financial position as at 31 December 20X8

	£	£	£
Net assets			
Financed by	Callum	Mark	Total
▼			
▼			

Picklist:

Capital accounts
Current accounts

BPP LEARNING MEDIA

Having completed Activity 1, a preparation-style question, we can move on to Activity 2. Activity 2 is representative of the style of question you may see in the assessment.

Activity 2: Anne, George and Timmy

This task is about accounting for partnerships.

You have the following information about a partnership business for the year ended 31 August 20X9:

- The partners are Anne, George and Timmy.
- The profit of the partnership for the year before appropriations is £182,000.

	Anne	George	Timmy
Profit share	45%	35%	20%
Interest on drawings	£1,800	£1,000	Nil
Interest on capital	£9,000	£5,400	£4,320
Annual salaries	£22,000	£12,000	Nil

You are asked to calculate the profit available for distribution for the partnership for the year ended 31 August 20X9.

Required

(a) Calculate the total interest on drawings for the year.

£

(b) Calculate the total salaries for the year.

£

(c) Calculate the profit available for distribution to the partners.

IMPORTANT: Show additions to the profit for the year as positive and deductions as negative.

Partnership	£
Profit for appropriation	
Interest on capital	
Interest on drawings	
Salaries	
Residual profit available for distribution	

You have now been asked to calculate the amount appropriated to Anne for the year.

(d) **Calculate the total amount appropriated to Anne for the year.**

IMPORTANT: Show amounts due to her as positive and charged to her as negative.

Anne	£
Interest on capital	
Interest on drawings	
Salary	
Share of profit or loss	
Total appropriation for the year	

8 Current accounts – further considerations

Generally, the partners' current accounts will be a credit balance (ie a positive balance).

This indicates that the profits appropriated to the partners are more than the drawings taken by them and any interest charged on the drawings.

However, it is possible that the current account will be a debit balance (ie a negative balance).

For example, this could arise if the level of profits appropriated to a partner is lower than the level of drawings taken in an accounting period.

Effectively it would mean that the partner with a debit balance on their current account owes money back to the partnership.

The current account is still shown in the financing section of the statement of financial position. However, it will be a **deduction** from the amount the partner has contributed to the business.

Illustration 5: Recording a debit balance in the financing section of a partnership statement of financial position

Jeff and Bill are partners in a partnership. The trial balance at 31 December 20X2 shows that Jeff and Bill's capital accounts and current accounts have the following balances:

Trial balance extract for Jeff and Bill as at 31 December 20X2

Account	£
Capital account – Jeff	20,000 credit
Capital account – Bill	40,000 credit
Current account – Jeff	1,400 debit
Current account – Bill	10,000 credit

Required

Complete the financing section of the statement of financial position for Jeff and Bill.

Statement of financial position for Jeff and Bill as at 31 December 20X2

	£	£	£
Net assets			68,600
Financed by	Jeff	Bill	Total
Capital accounts			
Current accounts			

Solution

Statement of financial position for Jeff and Bill as at 31 December 20X2

	£	£	£
Net assets			68,600
Financed by	Jeff	Bill	Total
Capital accounts	**20,000**	40,000	60,000
Current accounts	**–1,400**	10,000	8,600
	18,600	50,000	68,600

Explanation

This shows that the debit current account balance of £1,400 reduces the total amount owed to Jeff at the year end.

9 Changes to the partnership

We have studied the accounting treatment for existing partnerships. It is also important to consider the accounting procedures for a change in partners and the effect this has on partnership accounts.

As a partnership evolves, the business may need to admit new partners. Similarly, from time to time, existing partners will retire from the business.

A new partnership agreement will apply to the period after a new partner has joined the organisation or an old partner has retired.

The partnership agreement will reflect the partners' salaries that will be paid from the date the agreement takes effect, the rates of commission payable to partners, interest on capital, interest on drawings and the profit sharing ratio.

9.1 Admission of a new partner

As a partnership looks to expand the business, it may admit a new partner. This individual will be expected to bring finance and experience to the partnership.

The new partner will pay capital into the partnership and this will be credited to their capital account. The debit entry will be to the business bank account if it is a cash injection or otherwise an appropriate asset account.

9.2 Retirement of an existing partner

When a partner retires, they will be allocated their share of the profits which have accrued up to the date of retirement.

Once the profit has been appropriated, the retiring partner's current account needs to be updated.

The final balance on the current account will then be transferred to the retiring partner's capital account and this balance will represent the total amount they are owed by the partnership.

The balance owed to the retiring partner will usually then be paid to them in cash. If the partnership does not have sufficient funds and the retiring partner is willing to accept an alternative arrangement, the amount owed may be turned into a loan to the partnership.

The accounting entries required to settle the amount due to a partner retiring from the organisation will be demonstrated through the next activity.

Activity 3: Jennifer, James and Jonathan (part one)

You have the following information about a partnership:

- The financial year ends on 31 December 20X8.
- The partners at the beginning of the year are Jennifer, James and Jonathan.
- Jennifer retired from the partnership on 30 June 20X8.
- The balance on her capital account at that date was £60,000.

BPP
LEARNING MEDIA

Required

Show the journal entries that would be made if the amount owed to Jennifer was settled by a payment from the partnership bank account.

Solution

Journal entry

Account name		Debit £	Credit £
	▼		
	▼		

Picklist:

Bank
Capital account
Loan

In the activity above, the partnership has sufficient funds to pay Jennifer the balance on her capital account in cash.

This may not always be possible, in which case the partner will lend the partnership the balance on their capital account until it can be repaid.

The balance on the capital account therefore becomes a non-current liability in the statement of financial position and interest may be charged on this loan.

The interest is an expense in the statement of profit or loss and will reduce the profit for appropriation which is shared out among the partners in the appropriation account.

Activity 4: Jennifer, James and Jonathan (part two)

Using the information in Activity 3: *Jennifer, James and Jonathan (part one)*, assume Jennifer cannot now be paid the balance on her capital account from the organisation's bank account and so has agreed to lend this amount to the partnership in the form of a long-term loan.

- The financial year ends on 31 December 20X8.

- The partners at the beginning of the year are Jennifer, James and Jonathan.

- Jennifer retired from the partnership on 30 June 20X8.

- The balance on her capital account at that date was £60,000.

- Interest will be paid on the loan at a rate of 10% per annum; interest due is paid on 31 December each year.

- The net profit for the year to 31 December 20X8, before any loan interest, was £80,000.

Required

(a) **Show the journal entries that would be made if Jennifer agreed her capital could be treated as a non-current liability by the partnership.**

(b) **Calculate the revised profit available for distribution, after the loan interest has been deducted.**

(c) **Prepare an extract from the statement of profit or loss and statement of financial position to reflect the interest on the loan.**

Solution

(a) **Journal entry**

Account name		Debit £	Credit £
	▼		
	▼		

(b) **Revised profit available for distribution**

		£
Draft profit for appropriation per scenario		
	▼	
Revised profit for appropriation		

(c) **Statement of profit or loss extract for the year ended 31 December 20X8**

		£
Expenses		
	▼	

Statement of financial position extract as at 31 December 20X8

		£
Non-current liabilities		
	▼	

BPP
LEARNING MEDIA

Picklist:

Bank
Capital account
Interest charges
Loan

9.3 Goodwill

We are familiar with the statement of financial position and the net assets figure on the statement of financial position which shows the book value of the business. For example, Illustration 5 showed that at 31 December 20X2, the Jeff and Bill partnership had a book value of £68,600.

Often, however, the book value of the business differs from the price someone is willing to pay to acquire the business. They may be willing to pay more than the book value as a result of the perceived **goodwill** of the business.

Key term

> **Goodwill** is the excess of the value of a business over its individual assets and liabilities.

Goodwill may arise as a result of a number of factors, such as the reputation of the business or the skill of its management. It cannot exist independently of the business.

When a new partner joins the partnership, they will contribute capital to the business. This capital contribution often takes the form of a cash injection. Before the partner is admitted, the partnership must be valued so that all the partners know how much it is worth and can determine the amount the new partner should contribute.

Similarly, when a partner retires, it is important that they are paid a sum that represents not just the money they invested, but also their share of the extra value created in the business, ie their share of goodwill.

9.3.1 Accounting for goodwill in partnership accounts

As part of valuing the business, goodwill is calculated and then recorded in the partnership accounts on the date that a partner is admitted to the business or retires from the business.

Goodwill is an asset and therefore, when it is recorded in the partnership accounts, it is posted to the debit side of the general ledger. The corresponding credit entry is to the partners' capital accounts. It is shared between the partners according to the existing profit sharing ratio (ie the profit sharing ratio before a partner joins the partnership or retires from the partnership).

Journal to record goodwill in the partnership accounts (goodwill is recorded using the existing (or old) profit sharing ratio)

Account name	Debit £	Credit £
Goodwill	X	
Capital account – Partner A		X
Capital account – Partner B		X
Capital account – Partner C		X

Goodwill is an extremely subjective figure and so it is **not** left in the partnership's statement of financial position, but is immediately removed from the partnership accounts using the new profit sharing ratio.

Goodwill is removed from the partnership accounts with a credit entry to the goodwill account in the general ledger as the asset is decreasing. The corresponding debit entry is to the partners' capital accounts. It is allocated according to the new profit sharing ratio (ie the profit sharing ratio used from the date a partner joins the partnership or retires from the partnership).

Journal to eliminate goodwill from partnership accounts (goodwill is eliminated using the new profit sharing ratio)

Account name	Debit £	Credit £
Capital account – Partner A	X	
Capital account – Partner B	X	
Goodwill		X

The accounting treatment to record and eliminate goodwill will be shown in the next illustration.

Illustration 6: Goodwill

This task is about accounting for partnerships.

You have the following information about a partnership:

- The partners are Alan and Karen.

- Nick was admitted to the partnership on 1 September 20X9.

- Profit share, effective until 31 August 20X9:

    – Alan   35%
    – Karen   65%

BPP
LEARNING MEDIA

- Profit share, effective from 1 September 20X9:
  - Alan   25%
  - Karen   45%
  - Nick   30%
- Goodwill is valued at £90,000 on 31 August 20X9.
- Goodwill is to be introduced into the accounting records on 31 August 20X9 and then eliminated on 1 September 20X9.

Required

(a) Show the journal entry required to record goodwill in the accounting records on 31 August 20X9.

Account name		Debit £	Credit £
	▼		
	▼		
	▼		

(b) Show the journal entry required to eliminate goodwill from the accounting records on 1 September 20X9.

Account name		Debit £	Credit £
	▼		
	▼		
	▼		
	▼		

Solution

(a) Show the journal entry required to record goodwill in the accounting records on 31 August 20X9.

Account name	Debit £	Credit £
Goodwill	90,000	
Capital account – Alan (£90,000 x 35%)		31,500
Capital account – Karen (£90,000 x 65%)		58,500

(b) Show the journal entry required to eliminate goodwill from the accounting records on 1 September 20X9.

Account name	Debit £	Credit £
Capital account – Alan (£90,000 x 25%)	22,500	
Capital account – Karen (£90,000 x 45%)	40,500	
Capital account – Nick (£90,000 x 30%)	27,000	
Goodwill		90,000

Activity 5: Amy and Ben

This task is about accounting for partnerships.

You have the following information about a partnership:

Amy and Ben have been the owners of a partnership business for many years, sharing profits and losses 70%:30%, with Amy receiving the larger share.

On 1 September 20X8, the partnership agreement was changed so that Amy and Ben will share profits and losses 60%:40%, with Amy receiving the larger share.

Goodwill was valued at £110,000 at this date and has already been introduced into the partnership accounting records. It now needs to be eliminated.

BPP
LEARNING MEDIA

Required

(a) **Show the entries required to eliminate the goodwill from the partnership accounting records on 1 September 20X8.**

Account name		Amount £	Debit ✓	Credit ✓
	▼			
	▼			
	▼			

Picklist:

Capital – Amy
Capital – Ben
Goodwill

(b) **Complete the following statement regarding Amy's position in the partnership at the end of the day on 1 September 20X8.**

Amy's share of the profits and losses in the partnership has		▼
after the change in the partnership agreement.		

Picklist:

increased
decreased
stayed the same

10 Preparing a partnership statement of financial position

As we have seen, partners' current accounts and capital accounts are shown in the financing section of a partnership statement of financial position.

However, the net assets section of a partnership statement of financial position (the top section) is the same as the net assets section for sole traders.

Assessment focus point

In the exam, you may first be asked to calculate a specific balance to include in the statement of financial position (eg calculating the balance on the partners' current accounts). Then the requirement could be to prepare a statement of financial position from a trial balance. A proforma will be provided.

Activity 6: Fred and George

This task is about preparing a partnership statement of financial position.

You are preparing the statement of financial position for the Stone partnership for the year ended 31 August 20X9.

The partners are Fred and George.

You have the final trial balance below. All the necessary year-end adjustments have been made, except for the transfer of a £52,000 profit to the current accounts of the partners. Partners share profits and losses 30%:70%, with George taking the larger share.

Required

(a) **Calculate the balance of each partner's current account after sharing the profits.**

Indicate whether these balances are DEBIT or CREDIT (the answer fields are not case sensitive).

		Balance	Debit/Credit
Current account: Fred	£		
Current account: George	£		

(b) **Prepare a statement of financial position for the partnership as at 31 August 20X9.**

You need to use the partners' current account balances that you have just calculated in (a).

Do not use brackets, minus signs or dashes.

BPP
LEARNING MEDIA

Stone partnership
Trial balance as at 31 August 20X9

	Debit £	Credit £
Accruals		5,000
Administration expenses	20,621	
Bank		4,051
Capital account – Fred		25,000
Capital account – George		28,000
Cash	2,600	
Closing inventory	30,980	30,980
Current account – Fred		1,000
Current account – George	800	
Depreciation charges	6,000	
Discounts allowed	1,860	
Furniture and fittings at cost	82,000	
Furniture and fittings accumulated depreciation		10,000
Interest paid	420	
Irrecoverable debts	950	
Opening inventory	27,600	
Prepayments	2,300	
Purchases	200,030	
Purchases ledger control account		24,400
Rent	19,600	
Sales		373,121
Sales ledger control account	36,010	
Travel expenses	14,620	
VAT		5,239
Wages	60,400	
Total	506,791	506,791

Stone partnership
Statement of financial position as at 31 August 20X9

	Cost £	Accumulated depreciation £	Carrying amount £
Non-current assets			
▼			
Current assets			
▼			
▼			
▼			
▼			
▼			
Total current assets			
Current liabilities			
▼			
▼			
▼			
▼			
▼			
Total current liabilities			
Net current assets			
Net assets			
Financed by:	**Fred**	**George**	**Total**
▼			
▼			

Picklist:

Accruals
Bank
Capital accounts

BPP
LEARNING MEDIA

Cash
Current accounts
Depreciation charges
Expenses
Furniture and fittings
Inventory
Irrecoverable debts
Prepayments
Purchases
Sales
Trade payables
Trade receivables
VAT

10.1 Alternative presentation of cost of goods sold and inventory

As was discussed in Chapter 3 you may see cost of goods sold and inventory shown on two lines in the trial balance.

This means that the statement of profit or loss balances (opening inventory, purchases, carriage inwards and closing of inventory) have been totalled and shown on the cost of goods sold line.

There is a separate line for closing inventory. This is the asset which will be listed in the statement of financial position at the year end.

This question provides an opportunity to practise completing a statement of financial position under this presentation.

Activity 7: James and Mike

This task is about preparing a partnership statement of financial position.

You are preparing the statement of financial position for the Green Trade partnership for the year ended 31 May 20X2. The partners are James and Mike and both partners receive an equal share of the profits or losses.

You have the final trial balance below. All the necessary year-end adjustments have been made, except for the transfer of a £20,000 profit to the current accounts of the partners.

Required

(a) **Calculate the balance of each partner's current account after sharing the profits.**

Indicate whether these balances are DEBIT or CREDIT (the answer fields are not case sensitive).

	Balance		Debit/Credit	
Current account: James	£			▼
Current account: Mike	£			▼

Picklist:

Debit

Credit

(b) Prepare a statement of financial position for the partnership as at 31 May 20X2.

You need to use the partners' current account balances that you have just calculated in (a).

Do not use brackets, minus signs or dashes.

Green Trade partnership

Trial balance as at 31 May 20X2

	Debit £	Credit £
Accruals		955
Administration expenses	22,552	
Bank	5,356	
Capital – James		20,000
Capital – Mike		30,000
Cash	242	
Closing inventory	52,352	
Cost of goods sold	122,593	
Current account – James		400
Current account – Mike		650
Depreciation charge	6,353	
Disposal of fixed asset	424	
Motor vehicles at cost	66,324	
Motor vehicles accumulated depreciation		14,643
Allowance for doubtful debts		535
Change in allowance for doubtful debts	52	
Purchases ledger control account		85,130

BPP
LEARNING MEDIA

	Debit £	Credit £
Sales		205,452
Sales ledger control account	52,564	
Selling expenses	33,478	
VAT		4,525
Total	362,290	362,290

Solution

Green Trade partnership
Statement of financial position as at 31 May 20X2

	Cost £	Accumulated depreciation £	Carrying amount £
Non-current assets			
▼			
Current assets			
▼			
▼			
▼			
▼			
▼			
Total current assets			
Current liabilities			
▼			
▼			
▼			
▼			
Total current liabilities			
Net current assets			
Net assets			

	Cost £	Accumulated depreciation £	Carrying amount £
Financed by:	**James**	**Mike**	**Total**
▼			
▼			

Picklist:

Accruals
Bank
Capital accounts
Cash
Current accounts
Inventory
Motor vehicles
Trade payables
Trade receivables
VAT

BPP
LEARNING MEDIA

Chapter summary

- In a partnership the owners (partners) run the business together. They share the rewards of ownership (ie the profit) and also the risk of ownership (ie any losses).

- There are many similarities between accounts for a sole trader and accounts for a partnership. However, the allocation of the profit/(loss) is different and also the financing section of partnership accounts is different from the accounts for a sole trader.

- The appropriation account is used to allocate the profit/(loss) for the period between the partners. Profit can be appropriated through partners' salaries, commission, interest on capital and interest on drawings. Then the residual profit or loss will be distributed in accordance with the profit sharing ratio.

- The partners' current accounts are used to record the partners' day-to-day transactions with the partnership.

- The partners' capital accounts are used to record the long-term capital each partner pays into the partnership.

- Changes in partners have a significant effect on the accounts. The partnership agreement must be revised and the partnership accounts prepared on the basis of the new terms.

- Goodwill must be calculated and recorded in the accounting records when a new partner is admitted to the partnership or when an existing partner retires from the partnership.

- Goodwill is recorded by crediting the partners' capital accounts in accordance with the existing (old) profit sharing ratio and debiting the goodwill account in the general ledger.

- As goodwill is a subjective balance, it must then be eliminated from the accounts. The journal entry is to debit the partners' capital accounts in accordance with the new profit sharing ratio and credit the goodwill account in the general ledger.

- Once all necessary adjustments have been processed, the final accounts are prepared from the trial balance.

Keywords

- **Appropriation:** Sharing of the profit or loss which has been generated by the partnership between the partners

- **Capital accounts:** Accounts that record the long-term capital each partner pays into the business

- **Current accounts:** Accounts that record the partners' day-to-day transactions with the partnership

- **Goodwill:** The excess of the value of a business over its individual assets and liabilities. Goodwill may arise as a result of a number of factors, such as the reputation of the business or the skill of its management

- **Partnership agreement:** An agreement which establishes the terms of the partnership

- **Profit sharing ratio:** A ratio in which the profits or losses of a business are shared

BPP LEARNING MEDIA

Test your learning

1   Fred and George started a partnership business on 1 May 20X8.

   - The partners are Fred and George.
   - The financial year ends on 30 April.

Summary of the partnership agreement

	Fred	George
Profit share	75%	25%
Capital contributions made into the partnership bank account during the year ended 30 April 20X9	£32,000	£27,000
Drawings for the year	£20,000	£8,000

Profit for the year ended 30 April 20X9 was £50,000 before appropriations.

Prepare the capital and current accounts for the two partners for the year. Show the balance c/d at the end of the year.

Capital account – Fred

	£		£
▼		▼	

Capital account – George

	£		£
▼		▼	

Current account – Fred

	£		£
▼		▼	
▼		▼	

BPP LEARNING MEDIA

Current account – George

	£		£
▼		▼	
▼		▼	

Picklist:

Balance c/d
Bank
Drawings
Share of profit or loss

2   This task is about accounting for partnerships. You have the following information:

- The financial year ends on 31 August.
- The partners are Cedric and Harry.

Summary of the partnership agreement

	Cedric	Harry
Profit share	70%	30%
Annual salaries	Nil	£16,000
Capital account balances, 31 August 20X9	£60,000	£75,000
Drawings for the year	£24,000	£46,000
Interest on drawings for the year	£450	£760
Interest on capital for the year	£1,800	£2,250

The share of profit or loss for the year ended 31 August 20X9 was £90,000

Prepare the current accounts for the partners for the year ended 31 August 20X9. Show clearly the balances carried down.

- **You MUST enter zeros where appropriate in order to obtain full marks.**

- **Do NOT use brackets, minus signs or dashes.**

BPP
LEARNING MEDIA

Current accounts

	Cedric £	Harry £		Cedric £	Harry £
Balance b/d		500	Balance b/d	4,000	
▼			▼		
▼			▼		
▼			▼		
▼			▼		

Picklist:

Balance b/d
Balance c/d
Bank
Capital – Cedric
Capital – Harry
Current – Cedric
Current – Harry
Drawings
Goodwill
Interest on capital
Interest on drawings
Salaries
Share of loss
Share of profit

3 **Why should the rate at which interest is allowed on capital be included in a partnership agreement? Choose ONE answer.**

	✓
It enables partners to know the amount of profit available for distribution each year.	
It enables drawings to be calculated.	
It provides certainty over the value of the partnership.	
It means partners know the rate of return that they will earn on their capital.	

4   Alice, Beth and Emma are in partnership.

The existing profit share is:

- Alice   25%
- Beth   45%
- Emma   30%

Alice will leave the partnership at the end of the year. Goodwill is estimated to have a value of £110,000.

(a) What will be the amount of goodwill introduced into Alice's capital account at the time of her departure?

£	

(b) Will the goodwill introduced into Alice's capital account at the time of her departure be a debit or a credit to the goodwill account?

This will be	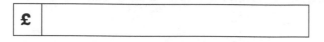	to the goodwill account.

Picklist:

a credit
a debit
no change

5   **Complete the following sentence by selecting the appropriate phrase in each case:**

When a partner retires from a partnership business, the balance on the		
▼	must be transferred to the	▼.

Picklist:

business bank account
partner's capital account
partner's current account

BPP
LEARNING MEDIA

Introduction to limited company accounts

Learning outcomes

2.1	**Describe the primary users of final accounts and their needs**
	• Know the primary users of final accounts
	• The reasons why final accounts are needed by these users.
2.2	**Describe the accounting principles underlying the preparation of final accounts**
	• Be aware of the existence of a framework within which accountants work
	• Know the underlying assumptions governing financial statements: accrual basis, going concern basis
	• Know the fundamental qualitative characteristics of useful financial information
	• Know the supporting qualitative characteristics
	• Know that financial statements should be free from material misstatement
	• Recognise circumstances when a business is no longer a going concern and be aware of the effect on the value of its asset.
6.1	**Describe the main sources of regulation governing company accounts**
	• Know the particular importance of maintaining an up-to-date knowledge of relevant legislation and accounting standards that apply to companies
	• Know which source provides the required formats for the statement of profit or loss and statement of financial performance for a company adopting IFRS
	• Know which standards provide guidance for property, plant and equipment, and inventories where IFRS is adopted (recalled as examples of regulation)
6.2	**Describe the more detailed reporting arising from these regulations**
	• Know the requirement to prepare financial statements at least annually and file them publicly
	• Know why selection and application of accounting policies is regulation, and the objectives that should be met when developing them
	• Know why limited company financial statements need to follow statutory formats, with prescribed headings and terminology
	• Know why cost of sales and other expenses must be classified according to rules
	• Know why taxation is charged in the statement of profit or loss of a company
	• Know why only the carrying value of non-current assets appears on the statement of financial position of a company
	• Know why notes must be provided as part of the financial statements of a company

Assessment context

Questions on this area will be tested in Tasks 4 and 6 of the exam.

Qualification context

The regulatory framework of financial statements is examined throughout your AAT studies.

Business context

The preparation of accounts from different types of organisation is the main source of revenue for a lot of smaller accountancy practices. An understanding of the regulatory framework is essential in order to complete the relevant returns in a timely fashion.

BPP
LEARNING MEDIA

Chapter overview

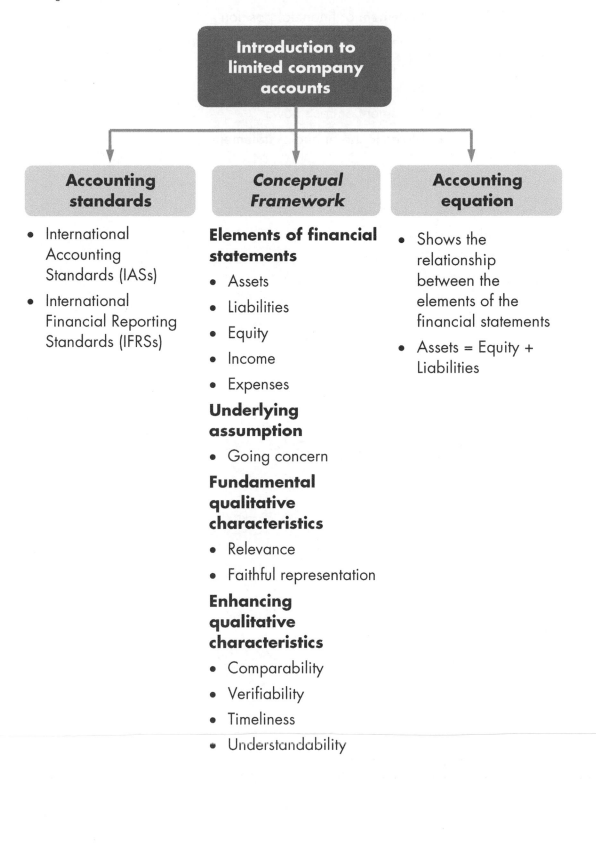

Introduction to limited company accounts

Accounting standards

- International Accounting Standards (IASs)
- International Financial Reporting Standards (IFRSs)

Conceptual Framework

Elements of financial statements

- Assets
- Liabilities
- Equity
- Income
- Expenses

Underlying assumption

- Going concern

Fundamental qualitative characteristics

- Relevance
- Faithful representation

Enhancing qualitative characteristics

- Comparability
- Verifiability
- Timeliness
- Understandability

Accounting equation

- Shows the relationship between the elements of the financial statements
- Assets = Equity + Liabilities

Set of financial statements

- Statement of financial position
- Statement of profit or loss and other comprehensive income
- Statement of changes in equity
- Statement of cash flows
- Notes to the financial statements

BPP
LEARNING MEDIA

Introduction

The regulatory framework

Limited companies are required to observe various rules and regulations when preparing financial statements. These regulations govern the accounting treatment of items and the way in which information is presented.

As we have seen, the purpose of financial statements is to provide useful information about the performance and financial position of an entity. Accounting regulations ensure that financial statements actually do provide useful information.

(a) Users of the financial statements need to be able to compare the financial statements of different entities and financial statements of the same entity over time. If preparers of financial statements were able to adopt whatever accounting practices they chose it would be impossible to do this in any meaningful way.

(b) Managers normally wish to show the performance of a company in the best possible light. Without regulation, information might be deliberately presented in such a way as to mislead users.

(c) The owners or providers of finance to a company are often external to the company and separate from its management. They depend on financial statements for information about a company's performance and position. Accounting regulations ensure that the financial statements provide all the information that users need in order to make decisions.

1 Generally accepted accounting practice (GAAP)

Limited companies are required to observe various rules and regulations when preparing financial statements. There are established national accounting procedures which are referred to as generally accepted accounting practice (GAAP).

In most countries GAAP does not have any statutory or regulatory authority or definition, but the major components are normally:

- Accounting standards (eg International Financial Reporting Standards)

- National company law (eg Companies Act 2006 in the UK)

- Stock exchange requirements (for companies quoted on a recognised stock exchange)

1.1 Accounting standards

Recent decades have seen a dramatic rise in global trade and cross-listing on the world's capital markets. This has led to significant demand for consistent international financial information.

Organisations set up in response to this demand are:

Organisations	Standards
International Accounting Standards Committee (IASC) Founded in 1973	Issued International Accounting Standards (IAS)
International Accounting Standards Board (IASB) Formed in 2001 and replaced the IASC	Adopted existing IAS Issues International Financial Reporting Standards (IFRS)

Accounting standards state how particular transactions and events should be reflected in the financial statements.

During this course you will study a range of:

- International Accounting Standards (IASs)
- International Financial Reporting Standards (IFRSs)

1.2 Sources of regulation

In the UK, the most important sources of regulation for limited companies are:

- Companies legislation (the Companies Act 2006)
- Accounting standards

1.3 What are accounting standards?

Accounting standards are authoritative statements of how particular types of transactions and other events should be reflected in financial statements. An entity normally needs to comply with accounting standards in order to produce financial statements which give a fair presentation of its performance and financial position.

It follows that unless there are exceptional circumstances, limited companies must comply with all relevant accounting standards. Sole traders and partnerships often adopt accounting standards, even though they may not be legally obliged to do so.

Although accounting standards state how particular items should be dealt with, many accounting standards set out principles rather than detailed rules. Preparers of financial statements should be guided by the spirit and reasoning behind accounting standards and not simply regard them as a set of rules to circumvent.

Two sets of accounting standards operate in the UK:

- UK accounting standards issued by the UK Accounting Standards Board (ASB). These are known as Financial Reporting Standards (FRSs).

- International accounting standards (IASs) or International Financial Reporting Standards (IFRSs) issued by the International Accounting Standards Board (IASB).

BPP LEARNING MEDIA

1.3.1 'Principles-based' approach

IFRSs are written using a 'principles-based' approach. This means that they are written based on the definitions of the elements of the financial statements, recognition and measurement principles, as set out in the *Conceptual Framework for Financial Reporting*. This will be studied later in the chapter.

In IFRS, the underlying accounting treatments are these 'principles', which are designed to cover a wider variety of scenarios without the need for very detailed scenario by scenario guidance as far as possible.

Other GAAP, for example US GAAP, are 'rules based', which means that accounting standards contain rules which apply to specific scenarios.

1.4 The purpose of financial statements

The purpose of financial statements is to provide information about an organisation's:

- Financial position (assets and liabilities)
- Financial performance (profit or loss)
- Changes in financial position (cash flows)

Users need this information:

(a) To make economic decisions (eg to assist in deciding whether to invest in the company)

(b) To assess the stewardship of the organisation's management (how well the directors have used the company's resources to generate profit)

Activity 1: Users of the financial information

Detailed below are some of the many user groups which have an interest in financial information.

What information would these users of financial information be interested in?

Solution

(a) Managers

(b) Employees

(c) Investors

(d)   Lenders

(e)   Suppliers

(f)   Customers

1.5 Conceptual Framework

The *Conceptual Framework for Financial Reporting* was produced by the International Accounting Standards Board (IASB). The main objective of this financial reporting framework is to provide the basis for:

* The development of consistent and logical accounting standards; and
* The use of judgement in resolving accounting issues.

(IASB, 2010)

This means that the principles of the *Conceptual Framework* are used by the IASB as a guide when producing a new accounting standard and used to minimise inconsistencies between standards.

The *Conceptual Framework* is also used to resolve accounting issues that are not addressed directly in an accounting standard. In the absence of a standard or interpretation, management must use their judgement to determine how to account for a transaction so that the financial information remains relevant and provides a fair representation. The *Conceptual Framework* should be used by management in exercising their judgement.

The *Conceptual Framework* is not a financial reporting standard and as such will be overridden if there is a conflict between it and a financial reporting standard.

1.6 Accounting principles

1.6.1 Going concern

The *Conceptual Framework* states that this is a 'fundamental assumption'.

The financial statements are normally prepared on the assumption that an entity is a going concern and will continue in operation for the foreseeable future. Hence, it is assumed that the entity has neither the intention nor the need to liquidate or curtail materially the scale of its operations; if such an intention or need exists, the financial statements may have to be prepared on a different basis and, if so, the basis used is disclosed.

BPP
LEARNING MEDIA

1.6.2 Accruals

The *Conceptual Framework* expects financial statements to be produced in accordance with the accruals concept.

Under the accruals concept the effects of transactions and other events are **recognised when they occur**.

This means that:

(a) Income and expenses are recorded in the financial statements when the business has **earned the income** or **incurred the cost** rather than when cash is received or paid

(b) Income and costs are matched to each other so that the cost of buying something that a business later sells is shown in the same financial period as the income from the sale (again, regardless of when the cash is received or paid)

(c) Items are reported in the financial statements of the period to which they relate

The accruals concept is also known as the **matching** principle.

1.6.3 Qualitative characteristics of useful financial information

The qualitative characteristics of useful financial information identify the types of information that are likely to be most useful to existing and potential investors, lenders and other creditors for making decisions about the reporting entity on the basis of information in its financial report (financial information).

The *Conceptual Framework* identifies two **fundamental** qualitative characteristics of useful financial information:

* Relevance; and
* Faithful representation.

Relevant information is information which is capable of making a difference in the decisions made by users. In deciding whether information is relevant it is necessary to consider the **nature** of the information and whether it is **material** in the context of the financial statements.

An item is **material** if its omission or misstatement could reasonably influence the economic decisions taken by a user of the financial statements.

Information that provides a **faithful representation** of a financial item or situation must be **complete**, **neutral** and **free from error**.

The *Conceptual Framework* identifies four further **enhancing** qualitative characteristics:

* **Comparability** – it must be possible to compare the results of different entities or to compare the results of an entity from one year to the next.

* **Verifiability** – the most useful information can be independently verified.

- **Timeliness** – information must be available to users in time to influence their decisions.

- **Understandability** – information should be presented clearly and concisely to make it understandable.

We noted earlier that there are many different user groups who are interested in financial information and that, while each user group has different specific needs, all are interested in the performance, profitability and security of an individual business.

Users therefore want to be able to compare the financial information of different businesses and so it is imperative that the accounting profession has a set of common concepts on which financial information is based.

1.7 Publishing the accounts

At present, unless they are quoted companies, UK companies have a choice when preparing accounts for publication:

(a) They can follow UK standards. This means that they must also follow certain rules set out in the Companies Act itself; these set out the format of the profit and loss account and the balance sheet, the accounting principles to be followed, and other disclosures that must be made.

(b) They can follow IASs and IFRSs. This means that they comply with IAS 1 *Presentation of Financial Statements*, which contains the formats for setting out financial statements under IFRS.

Quoted companies in the UK must prepare their consolidated financial statements in accordance with IFRS.

2 Financial statements for limited companies

2.1 IFRS financial statements

2.1.1 Presentation of Financial Statements (IAS 1)

IAS 1 applies to the preparation and presentation of general purpose financial statements in accordance with IFRSs.

This standard emphasises the general objectives of financial statements which are also outlined in the *Conceptual Framework*:

'The objective of general purpose financial reporting is to provide financial information about the reporting entity that is useful to existing and potential investors, lenders and other creditors in making decisions about providing resources to the entity.'

Conceptual Framework Chapter 1: OB2

IAS 1 *Presentation of Financial Statements* (para. 36) states that a complete set of financial statements should be prepared at least annually.

BPP
LEARNING MEDIA

A complete set of financial statements comprises:

- A statement of financial position

- A statement of profit or loss and other comprehensive income

- A statement of changes in equity

- A statement of cash flows

- Notes, comprising a summary of significant accounting policies and other explanatory information

In addition, the entity must clearly display:

(a)   The name of the company
(b)   The date of the financial statements
(c)   The currency in which the financial statements are presented
(d)   The level of rounding (eg £000 or £ million)

(IAS 1: para. 10)

2.1.2 Comparison with sole traders

The statement of profit or loss provides information about the financial performance of a business. It shows the income generated and the expenditure incurred during an accounting period.

You are familiar with preparing the statement of profit or loss for sole traders and partnerships, and many of the account names you have studied are also relevant when preparing company accounts.

However, certain headings are used when preparing company accounts. IAS 1 sets out the required IFRS formats for the statement of profit or loss and the statement of financial position.

2.1.3 Proforma – statement of profit or loss

XYZ Ltd
Statement of profit or loss for the year ended 31 December 20X2

	20X2 £000	20X1 £000
Revenue	X	X
Cost of sales	(X)	(X)
Gross profit	X	X
Distribution costs	(X)	(X)
Administrative expenses	(X)	(X)
Profit from operations	X	X
Finance costs	(X)	(X)
Profit before tax	X	X
Tax	(X)	(X)
Profit for the year	X	X

Note that the expenses are split into a number of categories – cost of sales, administrative expenses, distribution costs and finance costs. Cost of sales includes the expenses of manufacturing goods (such as labour, materials and factory costs) or the cost of buying goods for resale.

It is important that costs are correctly classified in order to allow users to compare the results of different companies in the same industry sector. For instance, if a company included some of its manufacturing costs under administrative expenses instead of cost of sales, that would overstate its gross profit.

In the case of a limited company, tax is deducted from profit for the year as the company must pay tax on its profits.

BPP LEARNING MEDIA

2.1.4 Proforma – statement of financial position

A statement of financial position shows the assets, liabilities and equity of a business at a stated date.

XYZ Ltd
Statement of financial position as at 31 December 20X2

	20X2 £000	20X1 £000
ASSETS		
Non-current assets		
Intangible assets	X	X
Property, plant and equipment	X	X
	X	X
Current assets		
Inventories	X	X
Trade and other receivables	X	X
Cash and cash equivalents	X	X
	X	X
Total assets	X	X
EQUITY AND LIABILITIES		
Equity		
Share capital	X	X
Share premium	X	X
Retained earnings	X	X
Revaluation surplus	X	X
Total equity	X	X
Non-current liabilities		
Bank loans	X	X
	X	X

	20X2 £000	20X1 £000
Current liabilities		
Trade and other payables	X	X
Short-term borrowings	X	X
Tax liability	X	X
	X	X
Total liabilities	X	X
Total equity and liabilities	X	X

While there are many similarities with the accounts for sole traders and partnerships, you will notice that company financial statements include some additional items, such as:

- Intangible assets
- Share capital
- Share premium
- Retained earnings
- Revaluation surplus
- Bank loans
- Tax

You will encounter these items as you continue your studies.

2.2 Notes to the financial statements

Notes provide or disclose information which is not presented in the statement of profit or loss and other comprehensive income, the statement of financial position, the statement of changes in equity or the statement of cash flows:

- Where it is required by other IFRSs

- Where additional information is relevant to understand any of the financial statements

Typically, many of the notes provide further analysis of the totals shown in the main financial statements.

Examples of items which are often analysed are:

- Property, plant and equipment
- Inventories
- Trade and other receivables
- Trade and other payables

BPP LEARNING MEDIA

For example, the note to 'trade and other payables' provides an analysis of this balance, and will show amounts arising from trade payables, accruals and other payables.

Items of property, plant and equipment are subject to an annual depreciation charge and this depreciation is charged as an expense in the statement of profit or loss. In the trial balance there will be an account balance for the original cost of items of property, plant and equipment and a separate account balance for the accumulated depreciation. When the statement of financial position is prepared, a net amount is simply shown, which is property, plant and equipment less depreciation. We refer to this as the 'carrying amount'.

The notes will include a property, plant and equipment note, which will show the various categories of asset and the relevant amounts of depreciation.

2.2.1 Accounting policies

Accounting policies are the specific principles, conventions and practices applied by an entity in preparing and presenting the financial statements.

The notes to the financial statements will also disclose the accounting policies adopted by the directors of the company. For example, they will disclose whether property, plant and equipment is held at cost or revaluation and how inventory is valued.

Companies should select accounting policies which give a 'true and fair view' of their financial performance and position. Accounting policies are determined by applying the relevant accounting standard. If there is no relevant standard, management should develop policies which result in financial information that is relevant and gives a faithful representation.

Companies are not allowed to change an established accounting policy without good reason and if a change is made, the financial statements for the previous year must be restated under the new policy, so that the results for the two years can be validly compared.

Activity 2: Qualitative characteristics

Indicate the *Conceptual Framework* qualitative characteristics that are being breached in these situations:

The directors have decided to move some expenses from cost of sales to administrative expenses this year.	▼
The accountant has produced explanatory notes which are very technical and nobody understands what they mean.	▼

Picklist:

Comparability
Timeliness
Understandability
Verifiability

There are two other standards that you should be aware of in addition to IAS 1:

2.3 Property, plant and equipment (IAS 16)

IAS 16 *Property, Plant and Equipment* sets out the way in which items of property, plant and equipment should be treated in the financial statements.

Property, plant and equipment are tangible items that:

- are held for use in the production or supply of goods or services, for rental to others, or for administrative purposes; and
- are expected to be used during more than one period.

(IAS 16: para. 6)

'Tangible' means that the item has physical substance.

2.4 Inventories (IAS 2)

Inventories include raw materials, work-in-progress and finished goods.

The basic rule per IAS 2 *Inventories* is:

'Inventories should be measured at the **lower of cost and net realisable value**.' (IAS 2: para. 9)

This is important as overstatement of the value of inventories will lead to overstatement of the company's profits.

2.5 The elements of financial statements

The *Conceptual Framework* defines elements of financial statements. The definitions reduce confusion over which items ought to be recognised and which should not (if an item is not one of the defined elements of financial statements it should not feature in the financial statements).

BPP
LEARNING MEDIA

The five elements of financial statements and their definitions are:

> **Asset**
> A resource controlled by an entity as a result of past events and from which future economic benefits are expected to flow to the entity.

> **Liability**
> A present obligation of the entity arising from past events, the settlement of which is expected to result in an outflow from the entity of resources embodying economic benefits.

> **Equity**
> The residual interest in the assets of an entity after deducting all its liabilities, so equity = net assets = share capital + reserves

> **Income**
> Increase in economic benefits during the accounting period in the form of inflow or enhancements of assets or decrease of liabilities that result in increases in equity, other than those relating to contributions from equity participants.

> **Expenses**
> Decrease in economic benefits during the accounting period in the form of outflows or depletions of assets or increases of liabilities that result in decreases in equity, other than those relating to distributions to equity participants.

(IASB, 2010)

The *Conceptual Framework* definitions demonstrate that IFRSs are based on a statement of financial position approach to recognition, ie income and expenses are defined as changes in assets and liabilities, rather than the other way round.

2.6 Recognition of the elements of financial statements

Recognition is the process of showing an item in the financial statements, with a description in words and a number value.

An item is recognised in the statement of financial position or the statement of profit or loss and other comprehensive income when:

(a) It meets the definition of an element of the financial statements; and

(b) It is probable that any future economic benefit associated with the item will flow to or from the entity; and

(c) The item has a cost or value that can be measured with reliability.

(IASB, 2010)

Hence, recognition relies heavily upon a good assessment of probability of whether economic benefits will flow to or from the entity.

2.7 Accounting equation

The relationship between these elements is shown by the accounting equation:

Assets = Equity + Liabilities

Rearranged: Assets – Liabilities = Equity

Equity = Contributions from owners + Income – Expenses – Distributions to owners

Therefore if net assets increase, it is either as a result of income or from a contribution. In the same way, if net assets decrease, it is either an expense or a distribution.

Activity 3: Elements of the financial statements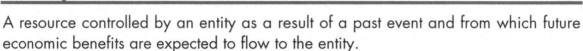

A resource controlled by an entity as a result of a past event and from which future economic benefits are expected to flow to the entity.

Required

(a) This statement describes:

	✓
An asset	
A liability	
Equity	
Income	
Expenses	

The residual interest in the assets of an entity after deducting all its liabilities.

(b) This statement describes:

	✓
An asset	
A liability	
Equity	
Income	
Expenses	

A distribution to equity participants is an expense.

(c) Is this statement true or false?

	✓
True	
False	

BPP
LEARNING MEDIA

Chapter summary

- Financial information must be presented fairly if it is to be useful. This normally means that it must comply with all applicable regulations.

- Regulations ensure that:

  - Users are able to compare the financial statements of different companies and of the same company over time

  - Users are not deliberately misled by the financial statements

  - Financial statements provide the information that users need

- The most important sources of regulation in the UK are:

  - The Companies Act 2006
  - Accounting standards

- International Accounting Standards (IASs) and International Financial Reporting Standards (IFRSs) are issued by the International Accounting Standards Board (IASB).

- The Companies Act 2006 states that the directors of a limited company must file annual accounts.

- Published IFRS accounts consist of:

  - A statement of financial position
  - A statement of profit or loss and other comprehensive income
  - A statement of changes in equity
  - A statement of cash flows
  - Notes

- **Accounting standards:** Authoritative statements of how particular types of transactions and other events should be reflected in financial statements

- **Asset:** A resource controlled by an entity as a result of past events and from which future economic benefits are expected to flow to the entity.

- **Conceptual framework:** A set of concepts and principles that underpin the preparation of financial statements

- **Equity:** The residual interest in the assets of an entity after deducting all its liabilities, so equity = net assets = share capital + reserves

- **Expenses:** Decrease in economic benefits during the accounting period in the form of outflows or depletions of assets or increases of liabilities that result in decreases in equity, other than those relating to distributions to equity participants.

- **Income:** Increase in economic benefits during the accounting period in the form of inflow or enhancements of assets or decrease of liabilities that result in increases in equity, other than those relating to contributions from equity participants.

- **Liability:** A present obligation of the entity arising from past events, the settlement of which is expected to result in an outflow from the entity of resources embodying economic benefits.

BPP
LEARNING MEDIA

Test your learning

1   We have mentioned that deadlines are important in preparing financial statements.

    Which of the enhancing qualitative characteristics of financial information as set out in the *Conceptual Framework* makes this clear?

    [▼]

    Picklist:

    Comparability
    Timeliness
    Understandability
    Verifiability

2   The IASB's *Conceptual Framework for Financial Reporting* is an accounting standard.

    Is this statement true or false?

	✓
True	
False	

3   **Which of the following items would appear in the statement of profit or loss of a company but not in the statement of profit or loss of a sole trader?**

	✓
Gross profit	
Cost of sales	
Profit before tax	
Revenue	

4   IAS 2 states that inventories should be measured at the lower of cost and net realisable value. This is to ensure that:

	✓
The accruals principle is applied to inventory	
Inventory is not overstated	
All the inventory has been accounted for	
Profit is not understated	

5 **Which TWO of the following correctly state the accounting equation?**

	✓
Assets – Liabilities = Equity	
Assets + Equity = Liabilities	
Equity – Liabilities = Assets	
Equity + Liabilities = Assets	

BPP
LEARNING MEDIA

Activity answers

CHAPTER 1 Organisations and their final accounts

Activity 1: Partnerships

	✓
Partnerships have a legal obligation to produce annual accounts.	
Partners are paid dividends from the partnership profits.	
Some partnerships have limited liability.	✓
Partnerships can issue loan stock to raise money.	

Activity 2: Incorporation

	✓
The sole proprietor will no longer have to pay personal tax.	
The sole proprietor will have greater control of the business.	
The business will operate in compliance with the Companies Act.	
The sole proprietor has more protection in the event of a liquidation.	✓

Activity 3: Limited companies

	✓
A company may only have a certain prescribed maximum liability on its statement of financial position.	
The shareholders of a company are protected in that they can only lose their investment in the company, should the company fail.	✓
A company can only enter into transactions involving debt up to a certain limit before gaining express approval from the shareholders in general meeting.	
The shareholders may only invest in a company up to a prescribed limit per shareholder.	

Activity 4: Duties and responsibilities of the directors

	✓
(ii), (iii) and (iv)	✓
(i), (ii), (iii) and (iv)	
(i), (iii) and (iv)	
(i), (ii) and (iii)	

Activity 5: Professional ethics

	True ✓	False ✓
Confidential information should only be shared with other accountants in your firm.		✓
The same audit team being sent to a client for several years can give rise to a familiarity threat.	✓	
Gifts from clients can be accepted as long as they are valued below £100.		✓

BPP
LEARNING MEDIA

CHAPTER 2 Incomplete records

Activity 1: Calculating sales as a missing figure

Sales ledger control account

	£		£
Balance b/d	1,447	Bank	39,204
Sales (β)	39,685	Balance c/d	1,928
	41,132		41,132

Activity 2: Calculating contras, VAT amounts and cash balances

(a) Sales ledger control account

	£		£
Balance b/d	22,000	Contra (β)	13,900
Sales day book	180,000	Bank	140,300
		Balance c/d	47,800
	202,000		202,000

(b) VAT control account

	£		£
Purchases day book	16,000	Balance b/d	5,780
General expenses	2,350	Sales day book	30,000
Bank	11,800		
Balance c/d (β)	5,630		
	35,780		35,780

(c)

£	104,206	debit

Workings

£83,456 + £150,300 − £129,550

Activity 3: Calculating purchases as a missing figure

Purchases ledger control account

	£		£
Bank	167,224	Balance b/d	38,450
Cash	430	Purchases (β)	173,029
Balance c/d	43,825		
	211,479		211,479

Activity 4: Calculating missing figures in general ledger accounts

(a) Sales ledger control account

	£		£
Balance b/d	10,253	Bank	50,424
Credit sales (β)	52,823	Irrecoverable debts	210
		Balance c/d	12,442
	63,076		63,076

(b) Bank account

	£		£
Balance b/d	923	Purchases ledger control account	27,432
Cash sales	14,440	General expenses	7,700
Interest received	180	Computers at cost	600
Sales ledger control account	50,424	Loan (β)	6,912
		Drawings (1,800 × 12)	21,600
		Balance c/d	1,723
	65,967		65,967

BPP
LEARNING MEDIA

Activity 5: Using margins to calculate missing balances

£	285,600

Workings

Sales	= 100%	476,000
Cost of goods sold	= 60%	285,600
Gross profit	= 40%	190,400

476,000/100 × 60

Activity 6: Using mark-ups to calculate missing balances

£	174,500

Workings

Sales	= 130%	221,000
Cost of goods sold	= 100%	170,000
Gross profit	= 30%	51,000

221,000/130 × 100

Cost of goods sold

Opening inventory	43,000
+ purchases (β)	174,500
– closing inventory	(47,500)
	170,000

Activity 7: The accounting equation

Assets = £	Capital £	+ Profit – £	Drawings £	+ Liabilities £
25,250 =	20,500	+ 3,100	– 1,600	+ 3,250

Workings

Assets = £	Capital £	+ Profit – £	Drawings £	+ Liabilities £
10,000 + 5,000 + 2,000 + 4,500 + 3,500 + 250 =	20,500	+ 3,100	– 1,600	+ 3,000 + 250
25,250 =	20,500	+ 3,100	– 1,600	+ 3,250

Activity 8: Missing balances and the accounting equation

(a) Capital account

	£		£
Balance c/d	16,400	Balance b/d	0
		Bank	15,000
		Purchases	1,400
	16,400		16,400

Explanation

The purchases are an additional capital injection as they are from the trader's personal bank account.

(b)

	Increase ✓	Decrease ✓	No change ✓
Assets	✓		
Liabilities			✓
Capital	✓		

Explanation

Assets increase by the proceeds from the sale and capital will increase from the additional profit made on the sale.

BPP LEARNING MEDIA

(c)

	✓
Direct debits on the bank statement have not been entered in the cash book.	
Cheques to suppliers sent out at the end of the month have not yet cleared.	✓
A receipt from a trade receivable has been posted to the bank account in the general ledger twice.	

Activity 9: Calculating missing balances and the preparation of final accounts

(a)

Assets (71,500 + 10,000)	£	81,500
Liabilities (3,200 + 16,100)	£	19,300
Capital	£	62,200

(b)

£	36,500

Working: 47,450/130 × 100

(c)

£	22,000

Workings

	£
Cost of goods sold	
Opening inventory	10,000
+ purchases	48,500
– closing inventory (β)	(22,000)
	36,500

(d)

This means that the inventory figures in the final accounts at 30 April 20X5 will be	
less than	the figure calculated in (c) above.

(e)

	✓
A bank overdraft	
Drawings that the owner has taken during the year	
Monies owed from a credit customer	✓
Monies owed to a credit supplier	

CHAPTER 3 Accounts for sole traders

Activity 1: Preparing final accounts for a sole trader

(a)

£	261,294

Tutorial working: 270,314 – 9,020 = 261,294

(b)

£	184,475

Tutorial working: 180,130 + 4,345 = 184,475

(c) Pearl Trading

Statement of profit or loss for the year ended 31 August 20X9

	£	£
Sales revenue		261,294
Opening inventory	18,311	
Purchases	184,475	
Closing inventory	–26,424	
Cost of goods sold	176,362	
Gross profit		84,932
Add:		
Disposal of non-current asset		510
Less:		
Carriage outwards	6,421	
Depreciation charges	9,524	
Wages	40,311	
General expenses	9,521	
Total expenses		65,777
Profit/loss for the year		19,665

(d) Pearl Trading

Statement of financial position as at 31 August 20X9

	Cost £	Accumulated depreciation £	Carrying amount £
Non-current assets			
Machinery	20,000	8,321	11,679
Current assets			
Inventory	26,424		
Trade receivables	38,310		
Prepayments	780		
Cash and cash equivalents	5,034		
		70,548	
Current liabilities			
Trade payables	30,300		
Accruals	5,310		
VAT	22,952		
		58,562	
Net current assets			11,986
Net assets			23,665
Financed by:			
Capital			
Opening capital			20,000
Add: Profit for the year			19,665
Less: Drawings			(16,000)
Closing capital			23,665

BPP LEARNING MEDIA

(e)

	✓
It shows whether the business has made a profit or a loss for the period.	
It proves that double entry has taken place.	✓
It shows which items belong in the statement of profit or loss and statement of financial position.	
It is produced automatically by a computerised accounting system.	

(f)

	✓
A newly purchased computer was not included in the physical count.	
The theft of a computer has not been recorded in the non-current assets register.	
The sale of a computer has been omitted from the initial trial balance.	
The purchase of a computer has not been posted to the general ledger.	✓

Activity 1: Callum and Mark

(a) Capital accounts

	Callum £	Mark £		Callum £	Mark £
Balance c/d	50,000	20,000	Balance b/d	10,000	7,000
			Bank	40,000	13,000
	50,000	20,000		50,000	20,000

(b) Partnership appropriation account

	£	
Profit for appropriation	50,000	
Salary – Callum	0	Enter any deductions as negative eg –999
Salary – Mark	–15,000	
Interest on capital – Callum	–800	
Interest on capital – Mark	–400	
Residual profit available for distribution	33,800	
Share of residual profit or loss:		
Callum (33,800 × 80%)	27,040	
Mark (33,800 × 20%)	6,760	
Total residual profit distributed	33,800	

BPP
LEARNING MEDIA

(c) Current accounts

	Callum £	Mark £		Callum £	Mark £
Drawings	6,000	8,800	Balance b/d	1,000	2,000
Balance c/d	22,840	15,360	Salaries	0	15,000
			Interest on capital	800	400
			Share of profit or loss	27,040	6,760
	28,840	24,160		28,840	24,160

(d) Callum and Mark
Statement of financial position as at 31 December 20X8

	£	£	£
Net assets			108,200
Financed by	Callum	Mark	Total
Capital accounts	50,000	20,000	70,000
Current accounts	22,840	15,360	38,200
	72,840	35,360	108,200

Activity 2: Anne, George and Timmy

(a)

£	2,800

Workings

£1,800 + £1,000 = £2,800

(b)

£	34,000

Workings

£22,000 + £12,000 = £34,000

(c)

Partnership	£
Profit for appropriation	182,000
Interest on capital (9,000 + 5,400 + 4,320)	–18,720
Interest on drawings	2,800
Salaries	–34,000
Residual profit available for distribution	132,080

Explanation

Interest on drawings is charged to partners and therefore added back to the profit for appropriation. Interest on capital and partners' salaries are appropriated to partners from the profit for appropriation. Therefore, they reduce the residual profit available for distribution.

(d)

Anne	£
Interest on capital	9,000
Interest on drawings	–1,800
Salary	22,000
Share of profit or loss (132,080 x 45%)	59,436
Total appropriation for the year	88,636

Activity 3: Jennifer, James and Jonathan (part one)

Journal entry

Account name	Debit £	Credit £
Capital account	60,000	
Bank		60,000

BPP LEARNING MEDIA

Activity 4: Jennifer, James and Jonathan (part two)

(a) Journal entry

Account name	Debit £	Credit £
Capital account	60,000	
Loan		60,000

(b) Revised profit available for distribution

	£
Draft profit for appropriation per scenario	80,000
Interest charges	(3,000)
Revised profit for appropriation	77,000

Workings

Interest charges: £60,000 × 10% × 6/12 = £3,000

(c) Statement of profit or loss extract for the year ended 31 December 20X8

	£
Expenses	
Interest charges	3,000

Statement of financial position extract as at 31 December 20X8

	£
Non-current liabilities	
Loan	60,000

Activity 5: Amy and Ben

(a)

Account name	Amount £	Debit ✓	Credit ✓
Goodwill	110,000		✓
Capital – Amy	66,000	✓	
Capital – Ben	44,000	✓	

Workings

Capital – Amy £110,000 x 60% = £66,000
Capital – Ben £110,000 x 40% = £44,000

(b)

Amy's share of the profits and losses in the partnership has	decreased
after the change in the partnership agreement.	

Activity 6: Fred and George

(a)

		Balance	Debit/Credit
Current account: Fred	£	16,600	Credit
Current account: George	£	35,600	Credit

Workings

	Fred £	George £
Current account balance per trial balance	1,000 credit	(800) debit
Share of profit (Fred: 52,000 x 30%); (George 52,000 x 70%)	15,600	36,400
	16,600	35,600

BPP
LEARNING MEDIA

(b) Stone partnership

Statement of financial position as at 31 August 20X9

	Cost £	Accumulated depreciation £	Carrying amount £
Non-current assets			
Furniture and fittings	82,000	10,000	72,000
Current assets			
Inventory		30,980	
Trade receivables		36,010	
Prepayments		2,300	
Cash		2,600	
Total current assets		71,890	
Current liabilities			
Trade payables	24,400		
VAT	5,239		
Accruals	5,000		
Bank	4,051		
Total current liabilities		38,690	
Net current assets			33,200
Net assets			105,200
Financed by:	**Fred**	**George**	**Total**
Capital accounts	25,000	28,000	53,000
Current accounts	16,600	35,600	52,200
	41,600	63,600	105,200

Activity 7: James and Mike

(a)

		Balance	Debit/Credit
Current account: James	£	10,400	Credit
Current account: Mike	£	10,650	Credit

Each partner is entitled to £10,000 of the profit which has been earned during the year (£20,000 × ½).

Before sharing profits, the balance in James's partners' current account is £400 credit. Therefore, after sharing profit, the balance in James's partners' current account is £10,400 (£400 + £10,000).

Before sharing profits, Mike has a credit balance of £650. Therefore, after sharing profits, the balance in Mike's partners' current account is £10,650.

(b) Green Trade partnership

Statement of financial position as at 31 May 20X2

	Cost £	Accumulated depreciation £	Carrying amount £
Non-current assets			
Motor vehicles	66,324	14,643	51,681
Current assets			
Inventory		52,352	
Trade receivables (W)		52,029	
Bank		5,356	
Cash		242	
Total current assets		109,979	

BPP LEARNING MEDIA

	Cost £	Accumulated depreciation £	Carrying amount £
Current liabilities			
Trade payables	85,130		
VAT	4,525		
Accruals	955		
Total current liabilities		90,610	
Net current assets			19,369
Net assets			71,050
Financed by:	**James**	**Mike**	**Total**
Capital accounts	20,000	30,000	50,000
Current accounts	10,400	10,650	21,050
	30,400	40,650	71,050

Workings

	£
Trade receivables	
Sales ledger control account	52,564
Less: Allowance for doubtful debts	(535)
Trade receivables	52,029

CHAPTER 5 Introduction to limited company accounts

Activity 1: Users of the financial information

(a) **Managers**

- Profitability
- Future prospects/plans to develop the business
- Current financial security
- Future financing needs/concerns
- Ability to pay a return to the owners (drawings/dividends)

(b) **Employees**

- Profitability
- Long-term growth
- Job security
- Likelihood of bonus
- Ability to pay retirement benefits/pensions

(c) **Investors**

- Profitability
- Future prospects
- Likely risk and return
- Chance of capital growth
- Ability to pay dividends

(d) **Lenders**

- Likelihood of repayment of capital amount
- Extent of other loans and the security of their debt

(e) **Suppliers**

- Likelihood of payment on time
- Likelihood of payment at all
- Whether they should continue to supply

(f) **Customers**

- Ability of entity to continue supplying
- Profitability as a measure of value for money of goods bought

BPP
LEARNING MEDIA

Activity 2: Qualitative characteristics

The directors have decided to move some expenses from cost of sales to administrative expenses this year.	Comparability
The accountant has produced explanatory notes which are very technical and nobody understands what they mean.	Understandability

Activity 3: Elements of the financial statements

(a)

	✓
An asset	✓
A liability	
Equity	
Income	
Expenses	

(b)

	✓
An asset	
A liability	
Equity	✓
Income	
Expenses	

(c)

	✓
True	
False	✓

BPP
LEARNING MEDIA

Test your learning: answers

CHAPTER 1 Organisations and their final accounts

1

	Profit making ✓	Not for profit ✓
A restaurant	✓	
A school		✓
A cinema	✓	
A public library		✓
A local council		✓
The Red Cross		✓
A church		✓
A bank	✓	
A public hospital		✓
A supermarket	✓	
An accountancy firm	✓	

2

(a) Sole traders and partnerships are **unincorporated** entities.

(b) **Public** limited companies can raise capital on the stock exchange.

(c) Directors manage a company on behalf of the **shareholders**.

(d) Duties and responsibilities of directors are set out in the **Companies Act**.

(e) The professional quality that requires an accountant to question information and data is **scepticism**.

3

	✓
Human error	✓
Lack of funds	
Hacking	✓
Malicious action	✓
Government interference	
Technical malfunction	✓
Intimidation	

4

	✓
Ownership and management are separated.	
Partners have no personal liability for the firm's debts.	
Each partner receives an agreed percentage of the profits.	✓
Partnerships can issue loan stock.	

5   This is a self-interest threat.

BPP
LEARNING MEDIA

CHAPTER 2 Incomplete records

1

£	72,900

Workings

Sales ledger control account

	£		£
Balance b/d	6,700	Bank (β)	72,900
Sales	69,400	Balance c/d	3,200
	76,100		76,100

2

£	127,000

Workings

	%	£
Sales	145	184,150
Cost of goods sold (184,150/145 × 100)	100	127,000
Gross profit	45	57,150

3

£	200,000

Workings

	%	£
Sales (130,000/65 × 100)	100	200,000
Cost of goods sold	65	130,000
Gross profit	35	70,000

4

£	15,300

Workings

	£
Opening net assets	58,900
Closing net assets	71,400
Increase in net assets	12,500

Increase in net assets   =   capital introduced + profit – drawings

£12,500   =   £10,000 + 17,800 – drawings

Drawings   =   £15,300

5

£	11,730

Workings

Bank account

	£		£
Balance b/d	1,020	Cash	37,100
Cash	48,700	Drawings (β)	11,730
		Balance c/d	890
	49,720		49,720

BPP
LEARNING MEDIA

CHAPTER 3 Accounts for sole traders

1

	✓
Inventories	✓
Trade payables	
Trade receivables	✓
Profit	

Explanation

Trade payables are 'liabilities' and profit is 'capital'.

2

	✓
£29,000	
£13,000	✓
£16,000	
£42,000	

Workings

Assets = £20,000 + £2,000 + £4,000 = £26,000

Liabilities = £3,000 + £10,000

Assets £26,000 less liabilities £13,000 = Capital £13,000

3

	✓
True	
False	✓

Explanation

Drawings are not an expense of the business. They are a reduction in the owner's capital, and therefore shown in the capital section of the statement of financial position and not as an expense in the statement of profit or loss.

4

	Cost £	Accumulated depreciation £	Carrying amount £
Furniture and fittings	12,600	5,920	6,680
Motor vehicles	38,500	22,400	16,100
			22,780

Workings

Depreciation charge:

Fixtures and fittings	(12,600 × 20%)	= £2,520
Motor vehicles	(38,500 – 15,500) × 30%	= £6,900

Accumulated depreciation:

Furniture and fittings	3,400 + 2,520	= £5,920
Motor vehicles	15,500 + 6,900	= £22,400

5

(a) Bernard Trading

Statement of profit or loss for the year ended 31 December 20X7

	£	£
Sales revenue		258,000
Opening inventory	16,500	
Purchases	196,000	
Closing inventory	–18,000	
Cost of goods sold	194,500	
Gross profit		63,500
Less:		
Carriage outwards	4,100	
Depreciation charges	24,000	
Loan interest	800	

BPP LEARNING MEDIA

	£	£
Miscellaneous expenses	2,000	
Office costs	2,400	
Telephone expenses	2,200	
Total expenses		35,500
Profit/loss for the year		28,000

(b) Bernard Trading

Statement of financial position as at 31 December 20X7

	Cost £	Accumulated depreciation £	Carrying amount £
Non-current assets			
Machinery	73,000	30,000	43,000
Current assets			
Inventory	18,000		
Trade receivables	64,600		
Prepayments	400		
		83,000	
Current liabilities			
Bank overdraft	13,300		
Trade payables	32,100		
Accruals	600		
VAT	12,000		
		58,000	
Net current assets			25,000
Net assets			68,000

	Cost £	Accumulated depreciation £	Carrying amount £
Financed by:			
Capital			
Opening capital			60,000
Add: Profit for the year			28,000
Less: Drawings			(20,000)
Closing capital			68,000

CHAPTER 4 Accounts for partnerships

1

Capital account – Fred

	£		£
Balance c/d	32,000	Bank	32,000
	32,000		32,000

Capital account – George

	£		£
Balance c/d	27,000	Bank	27,000
	27,000		27,000

Current account – Fred

	£		£
Drawings	20,000	Share of profit or loss (£50,000 × 75%)	37,500
Balance c/d	17,500		
	37,500		37,500

Current account – George

	£		£
Drawings	8,000	Share of profit or loss (£50,000 × 25%)	12,500
Balance c/d	4,500		
	12,500		12,500

BPP LEARNING MEDIA

2

Current accounts

	Cedric £	Harry £		Cedric £	Harry £
Balance b/d		500	Balance b/d	4,000	
Drawings	24,000	46,000	Salaries	0	16,000
Interest on drawings	450	760	Interest on capital	1,800	2,250
Balance c/d	44,350	0	Share of profit	63,000	27,000
			Balance c/d	0	2,010
	68,800	47,260		68,800	47,260

Workings

Share of profit – Cedric: £90,000 × 70% = £63,000
Share of profit – Harry: £90,000 × 30% = £27,000

3

	✓
It enables partners to know the amount of profit available for distribution each year.	
It enables drawings to be calculated.	
It provides certainty over the value of the partnership.	
It means partners know the rate of return that they will earn on their capital.	✓

4

£	27,500

This will be	a debit	to the goodwill account.

Workings

£110,000 × 25% = £27,500

5

When a partner retires from a partnership business, the balance on the		
partner's current account	must be transferred to the	partner's capital account.

CHAPTER 5 Introduction to limited company accounts

1 The relevant qualitative characteristic is **timeliness**.

2

	✓
True	
False	✓

3

	✓
Gross profit	
Cost of sales	
Profit before tax	✓
Revenue	

4

	✓
The accruals principle is applied to inventory	
Inventory is not overstated	✓
All the inventory has been accounted for	
Profit is not understated	

5

	✓
Assets – Liabilities = Equity	✓
Assets + Equity = Liabilities	
Equity – Liabilities = Assets	
Equity + Liabilities = Assets	✓

BPP
LEARNING MEDIA

Synoptic assessment preparation

The questions below are ones to consider once you have completed and passed your assessment. Thinking these questions through will enable you to consider the topics covered in the *Final Accounts Preparation* syllabus in a 'real world' context. This is a vital skill to develop before you attempt the synoptic assessment.

The questions presented are short-form questions. In the real synoptic assessment they will be attached to a wider case study.

Questions

1 **What is the objective of general purpose financial reporting according to the IASB's *Conceptual Framework for Financial Reporting*?**

2 **Give ONE example of a PRIMARY user of general purpose financial reports (financial statements) and explain their need for the information in financial statements.**

3 You have the following information about events on 1 April 20X6.

- A sole trader started business.

- The business was not registered for VAT.

- The sole trader transferred £10,000 of her own money into the business bank account.

- £800 was paid from this account for some office furniture.

- Goods for resale by the business costing £900 were purchased using the trader's personal bank account.

(a) Complete the capital account as at 1 April 20X6, showing clearly the balance carried down.

Capital

	£			£
▼			▼	
▼			▼	
▼			▼	

Picklist:

Balance b/d
Balance c/d
Bank
Drawings
Office furniture at cost
Purchases
Purchases ledger control account
Sales
Sales ledger control account
Suspense

At the end of the financial year on 31 March 20X7, you have the following further information:

- Total sales were £66,000.
- Total purchases were £59,120.
- A mark-up of 20% on cost was used throughout the year.

(b) Calculate the value of the cost of goods sold for the year ended 31 March 20X7.

4   You have the following information about a partnership:

Riva and Sam have been the owners of a partnership business for many years, sharing profits and losses in the ratio 3:2, with Riva receiving the larger share.

On 1 January 20X7, the partnership agreement was changed so that Riva and Sam will share profits and losses in the ratio 2:1, with Riva receiving the larger share.

Goodwill was valued at £72,000 at this date. No entries for goodwill have yet been made in the partnership accounting records.

BPP
LEARNING MEDIA

(a) Show the entries required to introduce the goodwill into the partnership accounting records on 1 January 20X7.

Account name	Amount £	Debit	Credit
▼			
▼			
▼			

Picklist:

Balance b/d
Balance c/d
Bank
Capital – Riva
Capital – Sam
Current – Riva
Current – Sam
Drawings
Goodwill

(b) Which of the following should be included in a partnership agreement? Choose ONE:

	✓
The partnership appropriation account	
Capital and current accounts for each partner	
Salaries and wages to be paid to all employees.	
The rate at which interest is to be allowed on capital	

Answers

1 The IASB's *Conceptual Framework for Financial Reporting* (2010) states that the objective of general purpose financial reporting is to provide financial information about the reporting entity that is useful to existing and potential investors, lenders and other creditors in making decisions about providing resources to the entity.

2 **Existing and potential investors**

Investors and potential investors need information to help them determine whether they should buy, hold or sell their investment. They need information which helps them to assess the ability of the entity to pay dividends and to assess the potential changes in the market price of their investment.

Alternative example:

Existing and potential lenders and other creditors

Lenders need information that helps them to make decisions about providing or settling loans. They need information which helps them to assess whether their loans and the interest attaching to them will be paid when due.

3 **(a)**

Capital

	£		£
Balance c/d	10,900	Balance b/d	0
		Bank	10,000
		Purchases	900
	10,900		10,900

(b)

£	55,000

£66,000/1.2 = £55,000

BPP LEARNING MEDIA

4 **(a)**

Account name	Amount £	Debit	Credit
Goodwill	72,000	✓	
Capital – Riva*	43,200		✓
Capital – Sam**	28,800		✓

*Riva £72,000/5 × 3 = £43,200

**Sam £72,000/5 × 2 = £28,800

(b)

	✓
The partnership appropriation account	
Capital and current accounts for each partner	
Salaries and wages to be paid to all employees	
The rate at which interest is to be allowed on capital	✓

BPP
LEARNING MEDIA

Glossary of terms

It is useful to be familiar with interchangeable terminology including IFRS and UK GAAP (generally accepted accounting principles).

Below is a short list of the most important terms you are likely to use or come across, together with their international and UK equivalents.

UK term	International term
Profit and loss account	**Statement of profit or loss (or statement of profit or loss and other comprehensive income)**
Turnover or Sales	Revenue or Sales revenue
Operating profit	Profit from operations
Reducing balance depreciation	Diminishing balance depreciation
Depreciation / depreciation expense(s)	Depreciation charge(s)
Balance sheet	**Statement of financial position**
Fixed assets	Non-current assets
Net book value	Carrying amount
Tangible assets	Property, plant and equipment
Stocks	Inventories
Trade debtors or Debtors	Trade receivables
Prepayments	Other receivables
Debtors and prepayments	Trade and other receivables
Cash at bank and in hand	Cash and cash equivalents
Long-term liabilities	Non-current liabilities
Trade creditors or creditors	Trade payables
Accruals	Other payables
Creditors and accruals	Trade and other payables
Capital and reserves	Equity (limited companies)
Profit and loss balance	Retained earnings
Cash flow statement	**Statement of cash flows**

Accountants often have a tendency to use several phrases to describe the same thing! Some of these are listed below:

Different terms for the same thing
Nominal ledger, main ledger or general ledger
Subsidiary ledgers, memorandum ledgers
Subsidiary (sales) ledger, sales ledger
Subsidiary (purchases) ledger, purchases ledger

BPP
LEARNING MEDIA

Bibliography

Association of Accounting Technicians (2014) *AAT Code of Professional Ethics. Version 2.* [eBook] London, AAT. Available from: www.aat.org.uk /sites/default/files/assets/AAT_Code_of_Professional_Ethics.pdf [Accessed 27 April 2016].

International Accounting Standards Board (2010) *Conceptual Framework for Financial Reporting.* [Online]. Available from: http://eifrs.ifrs.org [Accessed 27 April 2016].

IFRS Foundation (2016) *IFRS* [Online]. Available at: http://eifrs.ifrs.org [Accessed 27 April 2016].

International Ethics Standards Board for Accountants (2015) *Code of Ethics for Professional Accountants.* New York, International Federation of Accountants.

BPP
LEARNING MEDIA

Index

Private limited companies, 5, 16
Professional behaviour, 12
Professional competence, 12
Profit for the year, 74
Profit sharing ratio, 85, 118
Property, plant and equipment, 138
Public limited companies, 5, 16

Q

Qualitative characteristics, 131, 132

R

Registrar of Companies, 8, 10
Reversal of entries, 25

S

Self-interest threat, 12
Self-review threat, 12
Single entry error, 26
Sole traders, 4, 5, 16
Statement of cash flows, 133

Statement of changes in equity, 133
Statement of financial activities, 9
Statement of financial position, 41, 62, 74, 133
Statement of profit or loss, 59, 68, 74
Statement of profit or loss and other comprehensive income, 133
Statement of recommended practice, 9

T

The accounting equation, 24, 41
True and fair view, 9
Two debits/two credits, 26

U

Unequal amounts error, 26
Unincorporated entities, 4
Unlimited liability, 4

V

VAT, 27, 34, 44

BPP
LEARNING MEDIA

Notes

BPP
LEARNING MEDIA

BPP
LEARNING MEDIA

BPP
LEARNING MEDIA

REVIEW FORM

How have you used this Course Book?
(Tick one box only)

☐ Self study

☐ On a course_____

☐ Other _____

Why did you decide to purchase this Course Book? *(Tick one box only)*

☐ Have used BPP materials in the past

☐ Recommendation by friend/colleague

☐ Recommendation by a college lecturer

☐ Saw advertising

☐ Other _____

During the past six months do you recall seeing/receiving either of the following?
(Tick as many boxes as are relevant)

☐ Our advertisement in Accounting Technician

☐ Our Publishing Catalogue

Which (if any) aspects of our advertising do you think are useful?
(Tick as many boxes as are relevant)

☐ Prices and publication dates of new editions

☐ Information on Course Book content

☐ Details of our free online offering

☐ None of the above

Your ratings, comments and suggestions would be appreciated on the following areas of this Course Book.

	Very useful	Useful	Not useful
Chapter overviews	☐	☐	☐
Introductory section	☐	☐	☐
Quality of explanations	☐	☐	☐
Illustrations	☐	☐	☐
Chapter activities	☐	☐	☐
Test your learning	☐	☐	☐
Keywords	☐	☐	☐

	Excellent	Good	Adequate	Poor
Overall opinion of this Course Book	☐	☐	☐	☐

Do you intend to continue using BPP Products?   ☐ Yes ☐ No

Please note any further comments and suggestions/errors on the reverse of this page. The BPP author of this edition can be emailed at: lmfeedback@bpp.com.

Alternatively, the Head of Programme of this edition can be emailed at: nisarahmed@bpp.com

REVIEW FORM (continued)

TELL US WHAT YOU THINK

Please note any further comments and suggestions/errors below

CENTRAL BEDS COLLEGE
LIBRARY